Putting Diversity to Work

How to Successfully Lead a Diverse Workforce

Simma Lieberman, George F. Simons, and Kate Berardo

A Fifty-Minute™ Series Book

This Fifty-Minute™ book is designed to be "read with a pencil." It is an excellent workbook for self-study as well as classroom learning. All material is copyright-protected and cannot be duplicated without permission from the publisher. *Therefore, be sure to order a copy for every training participant by contacting:*

1-800-442-7477

Menlo Park, CA
www.crisplearning.com

Putting Diversity to Work

How to Successfully Lead a Diverse Workforce

Simma Lieberman, George F. Simons, and Kate Berardo

CREDITS:
Senior Editor: **Debbie Woodbury**
Editor: **Ann Gosch**
Assistant Editor: **Genevieve Del Rosario**
Production Manager: **Judy Petry**
Design: **Nicole Phillips**
Production Artist: **Rich Lehl**
Cartoonist: **Ralph Mapson**

© 2004 Crisp Publications, Inc.
Printed in Canada by Webcom Limited

www.crisplearning.com

04 05 06 07   10 9 8 7 6 5 4 3 2 1

Library of Congress Catalog Card Number 2003111222
Lieberman Simma, George F. Simons, and Kate Berardo
Putting Diversity to Work
ISBN 1-56052-695-5

Learning Objectives For:

PUTTING DIVERSITY TO WORK

The objectives for *Putting Diversity to Work* are listed below. They have been developed to guide you, the reader, to the core issues covered in this book.

THE OBJECTIVES OF THIS BOOK ARE:

❑ 1) To explain how diversity adds value to an organization

❑ 2) To present ways that organizations can support and improve their diversity practices

❑ 3) To help readers explore their own beliefs and attitudes toward becoming more open to diversity

❑ 4) To provide communication techniques and tools to help readers become diversity leaders

❑ 5) To explain how to recruit, hire, and manage employees of diverse backgrounds and cultures

ASSESSING YOUR PROGRESS

In addition to the learning objectives, Crisp Learning has developed an **assessment** that covers the fundamental information presented in this book. A 25-item, multiple-choice and true-false questionnaire allows the reader to evaluate his or her comprehension of the subject matter. To buy the assessment and answer key, go to www.crisplearning.com and search on the book title, or call 1-800-442-7477.

Assessments should not be used in any employee selection process.

About the Authors

Simma Lieberman: After completing facilitator training in New York City over 20 years ago, Simma was hired to improve working relationships amongst diverse racial and ethnic groups in and around New York. Today, along with a multicultural team, she helps her clients to create environments where people can do their best work and enjoy it. Simma Lieberman Associates is a multicultural organization offering a range of skills and experiences that are tailored to client needs. Simma's work includes speaking, coaching, training and consulting. She has written in and been quoted in publications throughout the world. *Simma@simmalieberman.com*

George Simons: Co-author of two other best selling books in this series, *Working Together* and *Men and Women, Partners at Work,* as well as of a new trade book, *EuroDiversity,* George has been serving both public and private clients worldwide for over 25 years. He is the developer of DIVERSOPHY®, the award-winning series of diversity and intercultural training games. George Simons International operates with a global network of professionals and specializes in *Intercultural Expertise Online.* *gsimons@diversophy.com*

Kate Berardo: As an intercultural specialist, Kate recently returned to the U.S. from Sapporo, Japan, where she was teaching cross-cultural competencies and English language skills. She is a summa cum laude graduate of Northwestern University (2001) who spent her undergraduate years counseling teaching assistants from Europe and Asia on cultural differences and effective teaching practices. She also developed the protocol for inclusive continuing education for the Center for Independent Futures in Evanston, Illinois, and worked as an editorial assistant on *EuroDiversity.* Her Web site, *Culturosity.com,* helps individuals develop intercultural awareness and build global careers. *kate@culturosity.com*

How to Use This Book

A Crisp Learning *Fifty-Minute™ Book* can be used in variety of ways. Individual self-study is one of the most common. However, many organizations use *Fifty-Minute* books for pre-study before a classroom training session. Other organizations use the books as a part of a system-wide learning program—supported by video and other media based on the content in the books. Still others work with Crisp Learning to customize the material to meet their specific needs and reflect their culture. Regardless of how it is used, we hope you will join the more than 20 million satisfied learners worldwide who have completed a *Fifty-Minute Book.*

Preface

Putting diversity to work in today's organization is everyone's job. Experience shows, however, that leaders who practice what they preach bring to life the rich human abilities of the diverse and global workforce more than any strategy or method can.

More and more, organizations are seeing that true success occurs on not just one, but on three bottom lines: *profit, people,* and *planet.* This book focuses on the business case and best practices for bringing the best out of all kinds of people. It is written for people who manage people and care for the places in which people work.

In a wired and global world, these places are not just offices and shop floors. They are communities, real and virtual, at home or spread across the planet. They are the communities that include our workers, our suppliers, our customers, and those public servants that manage our cities, states, and nation.

Putting Diversity to Work has four parts. We suggest for completeness that you read the book and do the exercises in the order in which they are presented. But if you must move from one part to another to look at issues that are important for you right now, start there and do the rest later.

This book gives you useful information and skills for managing successfully in a diverse workplace, but nothing contained here should be seen as legal advice or a legal opinion. The authors of *Putting Diversity to Work* have been careful to make sure that the content of this workbook is correct and up-to-date. But things change quickly in our fast-paced world. People, cultures, laws, and situations not only differ from one another, but they change. Make sure that you continue to research and use local and current sources of information. We are always happy to hear from you if you have feedback and new ideas.

We thank Leslie Berry of Chevron-Texaco, Marvin R. Smith of Marvin R. Smith & Associates, and Michael Stuber of mi•st [Consulting, who took the time to read our work and offer valuable advice. Thanks go also to Debbie Woodbury and all those at Crisp Learning who offered insights and help with the book's production.

Dedications

To my dearest friend Walter Painter Hopkins, who brings out the best in me in good days and bad. – *Dean R. Simons*

I would like to acknowledge my late partner Sandra Michele Brown, who helped me live diversity every day for 18 years, and son Avi, who continues to help me. – *Simma Lieberman*

To my parents, who planted the seeds of my curiosity and concern for people, and to my co-authors, for their mentoring and inspiration. – *Kate Berardo*

Contents

Part 4: Diversifying Your Workplace Successfully

Appendix

Making the Business Case for Diversity

With so much to think about at work, why focus on diversity? If you hear yourself saying, "I don't want to have to worry about anything else. I just need to worry about making money for my company," you may be missing the point. Having the skills to lead a diverse workforce will help your company increase its productivity and its profits. Today, it has become crucial for individuals and organizations to make diversity an important part of business strategy.

How does diversity sit with your fellow managers as a part of their everyday concerns? Make a guess—what percentage of them feel:

It's a high priority	Will do the basics	Nice if you have time	Not a concern at all
☐ %	☐ %	☐ %	☐ %

Employee Demographics

When the numbers and kinds of people in the population change, it means that your employee base is changing along with your consumer base. Globalization has you doing business with people from countries other than your own. If you do business the way you did in the past, you will not only miss new markets but you will lose out to competitors who know how to go after those markets.

Research done by DiversityInc.com shows that by the year 2008, women and people of color will make up 70% of new entrants to the U.S. workforce. How will your organization recruit and keep this new talent? What have you and your organization already done to make these people feel at home so they can be as productive as possible?

Creating a workplace where people from all backgrounds, regardless of race, ethnicity, gender, sexual orientation, age, religion, work, and communication style, feel included enables you to attract and keep all of your best people. It is expensive to lose good employees and have to hire new ones who might not stay if they sense that the company does not support their success. If employees feel that they are not valued or are discriminated against in assignments and promotions, it means loss of morale, downtime in productivity, and—so often today—even lawsuits.

What changes have you sensed in your workforce as a result of the changing nature of the population?

_____

_____

Marketplace Growth

In the 2000 census, 34.7 million people identified themselves as Black/African Americans. They are now 12.9% of the total U.S. population. People who identify themselves as Latinos or Hispanic are now 13.2%, or 35.3 million people. Research by the Selig Center for economic growth at the University of Georgia showed that consumer buying power will reach about $7.1 trillion, of which people of color will have 18% of that, or $1.3 trillion.

Gays and lesbians have $450 billion of buying power. Do you and does your organization now have the talent and resources to do business with these markets? Niche markets have repeatedly shown themselves to be loyal to organizations in which they see themselves represented.

If you do business with people who speak another language besides English, you need employees that also speak that language. They will help you create better relationships. They will make sure that your products or services are understood, and they can help ensure that you do not offend members of that market niche.

Can you afford to leave any group out? Employees from specific markets can help you market to those groups. And do not forget your own experiences and resources, because your own background makes you a part of different markets.

Check (✔) the groups below to whom your organization might improve its marketing:

❑ **Black/African Americans**   ❑ **Latino Americans**   ❑ **Gays and Lesbians**

❑ **Asian Americans**   ❑ **Other language speakers**   ❑ **Different age groups**

❑ **Native Americans**   ❑ **Pacific Islanders**   ❑ **Other:** _____

Putting Diversity to Work

Businesses that want to develop a competitive advantage now and in the coming years must use the power of diversity to build their business and increase market share. If they do not, they will be handing over profit, talent, and customers to competitors who understand and benefit from diversity. Putting diversity to work benefits organizations in the following ways:

> ### Recruiting the Most Competent and Creative
>
> As the workforce changes, competition for talent extends to all cultures, ethnic groups, and backgrounds. Qualified people will expect to see how committed you are to hiring and developing people from all backgrounds. They want to know that they are going into an organization that will welcome them and help them advance.

> ### Creativity
>
> People from different backgrounds, ages, genders, religions, physical abilities, sexual orientations, and thinking styles will solve problems more creatively and help you build business in different ways.

> ### Globalization
>
> To be successful doing business globally, you must have people that understand the cultures you deal with. As more organizations expand into the international market, you must see how the people in other countries see their needs and learn how they negotiate and create working relationships. Companies regularly lose business when they are not willing to understand other people or insist on doing things the way they do them "at home."

This book will help you see and use the bottom-line power of diversity.

Enabling Your Organization to Embrace Diversity

Some companies are figuring out that culture is not an obstacle to overcome. It is not something to manage, value, or appreciate—it's a resource and a lever to increase performance in the marketplace."

—**Patricia Digh, co-author of *Global Literacies***

2

Improving the Bottom Line Through Diversity

Diversity is rapidly gaining ground as a business asset. The demand for new customer-focused products, the desire to reach global markets, and the need to tap a diverse workforce for talented employees drives this trend. It may not be your job to build the organization's business case for diversity, but it is important to know how diversity can add value to your team, department, or division.

Leading companies today are beginning to realize that every business has to succeed not only on one, but on three bottom lines. A business must manage financial, human, and material resources in an ethical and sustainable way. It runs big risks if it does not pay attention to all three, as follows:

1. PROFIT ($) keeps an organization in existence, motivates its stakeholders, and enables it to invest in its future.

2. PEOPLE (☺) make an organization live and work, no matter how technical or automated it may be. People are our managers, our employees, our customers, and our communities.

3. The PLANET (🌐) hosts our enterprises and provides them with the energy and physical resources they need to produce goods and services.

Many people used to believe that as long as profits kept rolling in and the company kept growing, all was okay. No longer. Today we talk about employee satisfaction, investor confidence, environmental discrimination, sustainability, and many other critical people and planet factors that can make a company flourish or fall, whatever its apparent profitability at the moment.

Taking Advantage of Diversity in Your Organization

Research has shown that having a well-managed, diverse group brings advantages to all three bottom lines in the five ways that follow. As you read each item, think about your own organization. Note how you and your employees can use your diversity to contribute to each of the three bottom lines in each area.

Well-managed diverse organizations:

1. Understand and reach more diverse local customers and global markets for products and services.

$ _____

☺ _____

🌍 _____

2. Become known as a good place for all kinds of people to succeed, and act as a magnet that draws in diverse talent.

$ _____

☺ _____

🌍 _____

3. Draw from the wide range of experiences and perspectives to find more creative solutions to problems and be more innovative in developing products or services.

$ _____

☺ _____

🌍 _____

4. Become more productive. When an organization is diverse and inclusive, people feel valued rather than threatened and can be motivated to peak performance.

$ _____

☺ _____

🌏 _____

5. Reduce costs and contribute to increased profitability. Employees that are accepted and encouraged are likely to stay, reducing turnover costs and unnecessary talent searches. Less time is lost in grievances and legal actions. Company value increases, even in the stock market.

$ _____

☺ _____

🌏 _____

Identifying Your Stakeholders on a Mind Map

Inclusive and effective diversity leadership means involving *all* the important stakeholders in your organization's or group's activities. When you are aware of all your stakeholders, you can further integrate diversity into your business strategy. You make it possible for a larger consumer base to identify with you. You improve your reputation as a company that is inclusive in the way it does business. You gain more loyal employees who want to help you succeed. You respond to environmental challenges that affect you and your people as well as your profitability.

To help you identify your organization's stakeholders, diagram them on a "mind map." Begin by brainstorming with your colleagues all the categories of people, groups, and agencies involved in or affected by what your department or organization does or produces. Then draw the map, beginning with yourself and the people closest to you. Branch out to all the people, organizations, and systems that are affected by your work.

Put individual names in each category wherever possible. Sometimes this will be the person who has the most important role or carries the most influence in the stakeholder group you have identified.

Remember to keep this map up to date. New stakeholders may appear, others disappear, and the roles of the ones you identify are likely to change. Here is an example of what such a map might look like[1]:

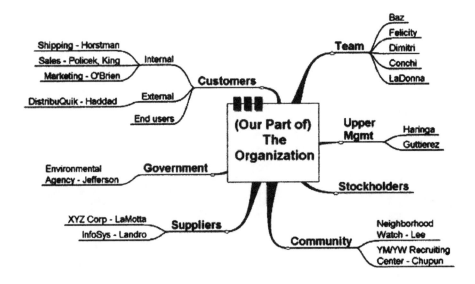

---

[1]Useful software for this kind of mapping can be found at www.mindjet.com.

Facilitating Stakeholder Synergy

The focus of this book is how diversity affects each stakeholder group and how diversity can be managed to everyone's advantage. Once you have named all the possible stakeholders, you are ready to take action.

The three-step process that follows will help facilitate stakeholder synergy, or compatibility, to support your diversity effort. With this process in mind, you can develop your business strategy with a diversity mind-set that will enable your organization to continuously gain a competitive advantage.

Assess   **A**nalyze   **A**ct

The table on the next page explains each of these steps in further detail.

Assess	Analyze	Act
Examine each of your stakeholders one by one. Mark which of them are:	*Do a force-field analysis of each stakeholder, starting with the most critical ones.*	*Act on your analysis. Provide each kind of stakeholder with the support needed to make progress.*
Champions – support diversity with enthusiasm. Go beyond what is technically required to make change succeed. Publicly make their commitment known. Need *support.*	**Ask:** • What forces support this stakeholder in his or her present level of involvement?	**For example:** • Let champions know you are behind them. Provide them with opportunities to leverage their commitment.
Collaborators – will not initiate but will moderately support the efforts and respond to requests with some amount of resources. Need *direction.*	• What forces might encourage this person to strengthen or to change position? • Which of these forces do you or others who support you control?	• Acknowledge collaborators' efforts and provide them a step at a time with clear objectives and tasks. • Use champions and collaborators to influence conformers and resisters.
Conformers – minimally support diversity by doing what is absolutely required by law or policy for compliance. Need *motivation.*	• What steps can be taken to move this person up the scale in the direction of becoming a champion?	• Make sure that passive resisters clearly know what is in it for them if they comply more readily and what the consequences are if they do not.
Uninformed – are simply ignorant of diversity issues and their role in them. Need *information.*	• In each case, which of these steps promises to produce the most change for the least effort?	• Provide user-friendly information for the uninformed via all available communications channels.
Passive Resisters – subtly or quietly oppose or slow down diversity efforts. Need *accountability.*	• Who is best positioned to take these steps or to support you or your team in doing so?	• Use networking and informal opportunities to encourage all stakeholders with personal support for change.
Active Resisters – strongly oppose changes supporting diversity. Likely to sabotage efforts by what they say and do. Need to be *converted or neutralized.*	• Are there efforts that need little time or resources and that might give you "quick wins" and produce a visible sense of progress? *Do these immediately!*	
Rank the stakeholders by the level of influence they have or might have on your diversity efforts ★ = small influence ★ ★ = moderate influence ★ ★ ★ = great influence		

INFLUENCING YOUR STAKEHOLDERS

Apply what you have learned so far to your own organization. Think of the next important initiative that your part of the organization should under-take. You can do this alone or ask your co-workers or team to try it with you.

1. Brainstorm and decide on an initiative that you feel should be under-taken. Write it in one complete sentence here.

_____

_____

_____

2. Create a stakeholder map.

3. Apply the AAA plan to the map you have drawn.

4. Even though this started as an exercise, what have you learned from it that you may be able to use?

_____

_____

_____

_____

Five Organizational Traits That Support Diversity

Today it is rare to find an organization that has not made some effort to respond to its own diversity and that of its local community and supply chain. How is your organization doing? Here are five essential organizational traits that support diversity initiatives and their *opposites* (indicated in italics)—characteristics of organizations that lack these traits. Diversity-supportive organizations:

1. **Act proactively.** These organizations know the value of diversity and the importance of tapping into it. They integrate the organization's diversity resources into everyday thinking and action. *Reactive* organizations deal with diversity only when they have to, usually when something has gone wrong.

2. **Are leadership-driven.** Top management endorses and actively champions the company's diversity initiatives. In *bottom-up* organizations, isolated individuals and groups see the need for diversity initiatives but must struggle for solid support from the top.

3. **Encourage ownership of initiatives.** When ownership is strong, all individuals in the organization are aware of and committed to carrying out their role in valuing diversity and making it work for the company and its people. In *compliant* organizations, people do only what they must to stay out of trouble. Compliance is important, of course, but it is only a starting point.

4. **Think inclusively.** Everyone is seen as part of the organization's diversity. All have the responsibility to give to and receive from the diversity effort. *Competitive* thinking tends to pit one group against another and stay focused only on special interests. Most organizations must recognize the neglected interests of some of their groups, as a normal part of starting to make diversity work, but the goal is to make everyone's needs and concerns a part of the mainstream diversity effort.

5. **Mainstream diversity.** These organizations make diversity a part of every effort. Although the organization may have some specialized diversity training courses, diversity considerations are a normal part of every training program, an explicit part of every approach to customers and community. In *fragmented* organizations, diversity may be something everyone should be exposed to, but it may or may not be considered in other educational efforts or in everyday operational decisions.

WHERE DOES YOUR ORGANIZATION STAND NOW?

Use the scales below to show the progress your organization is making and the direction in which it needs to go. Using the five preceding definitions, place an X at the point on the scale that you believe best describes your organization. Then note in the space below the evidence or behaviors that tell you this is so.

1. My organization acts:

Proactively————+————+————+————+————**Reactively**

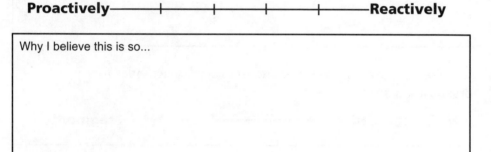

Why I believe this is so...

2. In my organization, diversity is:

Leadership-driven————+————+————+————+————**Bottom-up**

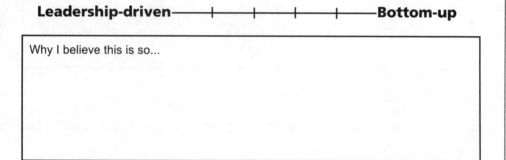

Why I believe this is so...

3. In my organization's diversity activities, I see mostly:

Ownership————+————+————+————+————**Compliance**

Why I believe this is so...

————CONTINUED————

4. Divesity thinking in my organization is:

Inclusive———+———+———+———+———**Competitive**

Why I believe this is so...

5. Diversity concerns in learning and in everyday activities in my organization are:

Mainstreamed———+———+———+———+———**Fragmented**

Why I believe this is so...

Diversifying Your Organization's Supply Chain

Supplier diversity is becoming a separate responsibility within purchasing in many companies, notes Richard J. Hernández, CPCM (www.e-mbe.net/February 2001). He advises that minority-owned and women-owned suppliers are less likely to get overlooked when the purchasing organization implements these recommendations:

➢ **Have a proactive outreach program,** including such activities as attending trade fairs and advertising locally. Make yourself available via the Internet or an extranet that attracts supplier diversity.

➢ **Set quantifiable goals** to which managers and individual buyers are held accountable in their performance appraisals just as they are for cost savings, product or service quality, and reduced procurement lead time. An awards program can recognize individuals who make the extra effort and encourage others.

➢ **Educate buyers and prime suppliers** to develop and manage supplier diversity programs so that subcontractors also benefit. Pre-source by determining potential areas of need and locating potential suppliers to meet them. Use this normal part of effective supply chain management to focus on buyer diversity. It makes your buying proactive and gives diverse suppliers a fair chance to compete.

➢ **Train and mentor** smaller and diverse suppliers for e-commerce. Diverse firms can benefit from these new developments, but only if they are brought aboard as these radical changes occur in supply management.

➢ **Use third-party certified suppliers** to avoid "front" companies that pretend to be woman- or minority-owned.

Marvin R. Smith of Marvin R. Smith & Associates, who spent several years developing and managing the supplier management program at the Lawrence Livermore National Laboratory, strongly suggests that the most effective way for an organization to achieve and maintain supplier diversity is by managing *all* suppliers on an ongoing basis, rather than taking a per-transaction approach.

Benchmarking to Improve Diversity Practices

Now that you have analyzed to what degree your organization supports diversity, you have probably seen areas in which it could improve. There is no single or perfect formula for making diversity into an asset, but the exchange of best practices between companies and organizations can help enormously. This is called *benchmarking*. When applied in and across industries and sectors, benchmarking can help you find the best directions for your company's efforts and your own.

Proactive organizations use benchmarking to search actively for best practices and high performance standards. Then they measure their actual business processes and operations against those standards. Benchmarking diversity efforts across industries helps organizations reach their diversity goals more creatively and effectively.

Perhaps your organization already belongs to a diversity benchmarking group. If not, many benchmarking results and best practices can be found in diversity publications and on the Internet. They may also be among the activities of professional groups to which you or others in your company belong. Benchmarking allows you to learn from the best diversity practices of others and to share those that people in your organization have developed.

Six Criteria for Best Practices

Benchmarking is about finding out what people are doing that really works, identifying what are called *best practices*. An activity is most likely to succeed if it meets the criteria listed below.

➤ It has worked successfully over a period of time.

➤ You can measure the quantity or quality of the results.

➤ It gives other identifiable positive results, such as employee or customer satisfaction, or change in organizational behavior.

➤ It adds value by improving service, quality, or productivity.

➤ It takes a fresh or innovative approach to producing the result.

➤ It can be modified and transferred to other organizations.

WHAT IS HAPPENING IN YOUR ORGANIZATION?

What practices are being used in parts of your organization that could be broadened, used elsewhere, or adapted to improve diversity performance? See if you can identify one such practice in each of the following categories.

1. Challenging ideas and outlooks:

_____

_____

_____

2. Processes that some groups have adopted:

_____

_____

_____

3. Things being done and said by leaders and others who champion diversity effectively:

_____

_____

_____

Listed below are the six criteria you just learned for a diversity best practice. The boxes on the right represent the three practices you described above. Check (✓) the boxes where each practice meets the criteria.

	1.	2.	3.
Has it worked successfully over a period of time?	❏	❏	❏
Can you measure the quantitative or qualitative results?	❏	❏	❏
Has it yielded other identifiable positive results, such as employee or customer satisfaction, change in organizational behavior, or another positive impact?	❏	❏	❏
Does it add value by improving service, quality, or productivity?	❏	❏	❏
Does it involve a fresh or innovative approach to producing the result?	❏	❏	❏
Can it be modified and transferred to other organizations?	❏	❏	❏

Embracing Diversity Strategies from Benchmarking

Benchmarking across industries and sectors has led to the identification of strategies, outlined below, for effectively putting diversity to work. You will recognize these strategies as the organizational traits that support diversity, which you learned earlier. Which of these could you or your organization adapt or adopt? What ideas come to you from seeing what other organizations are doing? Note your own ideas after each item.

1. Becoming Proactive

Make sure that the business case for diversity is in place and that the organizational mission statement strongly makes the case for the value that diversity will add to the organization's activities.

Example: *Top managers of a leading building materials manufacturer took two days out to create a "Business Case" promoting the diversity initiative throughout the corporation, making diversity one of the organization's six core values.*

_____

_____

2. Exercising Leadership

Create a strategic plan that includes measurable diversity goals for each business unit with a high-level manager responsible for achieving them.

Example: *Walk the talk. The CEO of one of the world's largest soft drink manufacturers tied his own compensation, and that of his managers, to achievement of their diversity goals.*

_____

_____

3. Increasing Ownership

Use a company- or division-wide event to involve all employees in sharing their experiences, hopes, and ideas for diversity or about an important diversity issue. Large group learning and planning approaches such as *Appreciative Inquiry* can be useful for this.[2]

Example: *A multinational cosmetics manufacturer sponsored a division-wide event for "men and women working together in teams," which brought out best practices and fostered appointment of women at the executive level.*

_____

_____

4. Fostering Inclusivity

Make sure that diversity is about benefiting all people in the organization according to their diverse needs.

Example: *A major automobile manufacturer has created a work/family account for each salaried employee, providing an annual sum of money that the employee is free to use for child care, adoption, dependent education, elder care, or retirement. The allocation increases with each year of service until a limit is reached.*

_____

_____

5. Mainstreaming Diversity

Communicate constantly. Mention diversity as a matter of course in formal and informal communications—written, spoken, and online—in trainings, presentations, and speeches. Make sure these messages tell about the success of or progress made on specific diversity goals.

Example: *A global pharmaceutical company has appointed a traveling team of facilitators whose job is to gather and spread best practices throughout the organization. Cultural competence and diversity management are a normal part of their examination of all best practices.*

_____

_____

Review your notes and ideas. Which ones are you most ready to share with others or to act on? When will you do that?

Idea   **When to act on it**

_____   _____

_____   _____

You also can ask your employees for input. Ask what best practices have worked for them. Offer an incentive to employees who contribute best practices they have seen or done. Involve everyone at all levels of your organization so everyone can learn and be part of the diversity initiative.

_____
[2]J.M. Watkins and Bernard Mohr, *Appreciative Inquiry: Change at the Speed of Imagination* (New York: John Wiley & Sons, 2001).

Return on Invested Capital (ROIC)

Diversity pays off on many levels. The ROIC acronym underscores the characteristics of a successful diversity initiative. How present are they in your organization? Note your responses to the right.

Relevant

Our diversity effort fits the needs of our diverse people and their roles in the organization. It also helps them meet the organization's goals and objectives. We deal in a culturally fitting way with all parts of our population. We act from our common vision and express our efforts in our own stories and images.

Owned by All

The program belongs to all of us, not just to management, HR, or other professionals. We all create best practices and see ourselves as responsible for seeing and meeting our diversity needs. Diversity is a proud part of our organization's culture. People don't just preach the program's values to each other; they live them.

Inclusive

Diversity aims at getting 100% success from 100% of our people. Although some groups must focus on their own specific needs, we are all allies for each other. Old and young, leaders and workers, men and women—not just the marginalized— serve and have access to service. Individuals connect to each other across cultural boundaries.

Complete

We pay attention to all four tasks of diversity: achieving justice, reducing bias, becoming culturally competent, and using our diversity to add value. Diversity is integrated into all our programs, systems, and activities. It is how we do all that we do, not a special activity.

Recognizing the Signs of Success

Not everything can be measured immediately in ROIC, but there are indicators that diversity thinking is taking hold in an organization. Canadian diversity specialists Glen and Helgi Eyford offer the following clues.[3] As you read them or discuss them with your colleagues, think about your organization. What level has diversity thinking reached? What might be missing?

➤ There is broad participation in the effort, such as among leaders and workers, men and women, young and old, and so on.

little or none > > > > > > > **some** > > > > > > > **normal for us**

➤ The influence of diversity thinking is found in most programs, systems, and activities. Diversity is no longer just a special activity.

little or none > > > > > > > **some** > > > > > > > **normal for us**

➤ Talking about diversity issues and differences is valued and ongoing. It shows up in the decision-making of formal and informal groups and teams.

little or none > > > > > > > **some** > > > > > > > **normal for us**

➤ People own the effort and are creating their own ways of valuing and using their diversity. Ideas come from every quarter, not just from HR or the diversity committee or an outside consultant.

little or none > > > > > > > **some** > > > > > > > **normal for us**

➤ The organization is making resources available—such as budget, time, and learning opportunities—for diversity concerns.

little or none > > > > > > > **some** > > > > > > > **normal for us**

➤ Individuals and groups in the organization recognize diverse needs and volunteer their own resources to meet them.

little or none > > > > > > > **some** > > > > > > > **normal for us**

➤ People model diversity thinking and behavior for each other, rather than just preaching it to the "unsaved."

little or none > > > > > > > **some** > > > > > > > **normal for us**

➤ Diversity shows up in the artifacts of the organization's groups and is a recognizable current in the environment: posters, bulletin boards, art, celebrations, "folk art," and more.

little or none > > > > > > > some > > > > > > > normal for us

➤ Real connections, collaborations, and friendships are forming across cultural boundaries.

little or none > > > > > > > some > > > > > > > normal for us

What other signs of success have you noticed in your organization to add to this list?

_____

_____

_____

_____

Put a tickler to this exercise in your agenda for six months from now to see if your answers show a growth in your organization's diversity thinking and behavior.

---

[3] Adapted from *Involving Culture: A Fieldworker's Guide to Culturally Sensitive Development*. (Ottawa: Canadian International Development Agency, 1995.)

Develop Yourself to Embrace Diversity

" *There is nothing in the world as interesting as people, and one can never study them enough.*"

—Vincent van Gogh, Dutch Post-Impressionist Painter

Common Ideas About Diversity

This part helps you develop yourself by letting you look at what you believe and how you act about diversity. How do the following statements strike you?

➤ *"Diversity is really about women and minorities."*

➤ *"Diversity training is just another passing business trend."*

➤ *"I'm not prejudiced."*

➤ *"Diversity concerns human resources, not line managers."*

➤ *"The best way to deal with diversity is to just follow laws and policies."*

➤ *"Just treat everyone the same and there will be no problem."*

➤ *"Talking about diversity only separates us further."*

Would it surprise you to know that *all* of these statements are false? By the end of Part 2, you will know why. In this part you will:

➤ Look at what diversity is and why it is important

➤ See how diversity is present in your organization

➤ Learn more about yourself and what influences you

➤ Recognize how diversity can help you as a person and as a manager

➤ Prepare yourself mentally to value and manage diversity

➤ Develop an approach for dealing with diversity-related situations

➤ Apply your personal development to your role as a manager

What Exactly *Is* Diversity?

Diversity looks at the differences that shape people's thinking and behavior. What comes to mind when you think of diversity? Inside this box, write the first five or six things you think of:

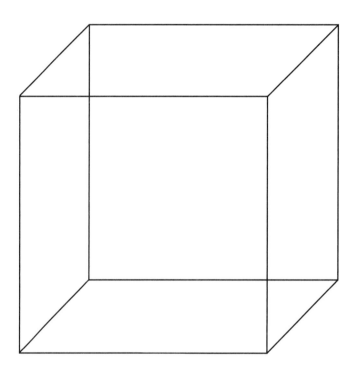

Now ask yourself, "How else do people differ?" Think of as many things as you can and write them *outside* the box. How many can you think of? When we talk about diversity, we mean all of the differences that affect how we think, act, and communicate. No matter how many breaths we take, we will not be able to name all these differences because they change with each interaction.

You and your boss may be from different countries. You may have different ways of speaking, different ideas about how to manage a company, and different sexual orientations. The last employee you spoke to could be at a different stage in her life, have a different religion, and work under different money pressures than you do.

All these differences affect how each of us thinks and acts and can greatly influence how, when, and with whom we communicate. Therefore, it is better to include more differences rather than fewer when thinking about diversity.

Thinking Outside the Box

Developing yourself means stepping back from your ideas to think about how you got them in the first place and what they really mean. In this sense, your head is like a box. Inside, you carry certain ideas and thoughts that you do not stop to think about. Thinking "outside the box" means taking what we usually expect to be true or right and looking at it from other points of view.

What you wrote outside the box above were things that you did not automatically connect with diversity but that came to mind when you were asked to think about how people can be different. Understanding diversity means moving *into* the box all these ideas, and the ones that others make you aware of, so that you start thinking of diversity as many differences, not just the most apparent ones.

> Valuing diversity means seeing the value found in our differences and welcoming different thoughts, perspectives, and people into how we live and work.

66 Ways We Differ[4]

1. What we call "proper" behavior

2. How and when we greet each other

3. What is common courtesy

4. What is polite and impolite

5. How close we stand to each other

6. What holidays we celebrate and how we celebrate them

7. How we show respect and disrespect

8. How and when we use money, credit, and bartering

9. The range in which we negotiate

10. What is modest or risqué

11. What is embarrassing or shameful

12. What makes us feel good and what depresses us

13. What makes us proud and what shames us

14. What, when, and how we eat or drink

15. What we wear, and when and where we wear it

16. How we see and behave toward sickness and health

17. How and when we seek and use health services

18. What we find funny or sad

19. How and when we use transportation

20. What we buy and sell—when, how, and with whom we do it

21. When, where, how we sit or stand

22. If, how, when we touch each other

23. What we believe

24. What we value

25. What makes "common sense"

---

[4] Adapted from *Global Competence: 50 Exercises for Succeeding in International Business,* edited by George Simons, Selma Myers, and Jonamay Lambert, HRD Press, 2000. Available at www.diversophy.com.

26. What are worthwhile goals in life

27. What is beautiful or ugly

28. The nature of God and other religious beliefs

29. What we believe we need and do not need

30. When privacy is desirable

31. Whether a person feels in control of life or whether fate determines it

32. Who makes what decisions and in what circumstances

33. What should be communicated directly or indirectly

34. What or who is clean or dirty

35. What language, dialect, and tone of voice we use

36. To whom we speak and to whom we do not

37. The role of the individual

38. The roles of men and women and how each should behave

39. The roles of parents and children and how each should behave

40. How important harmony is in a group

41. How important competition is between individuals

42. Social class

43. Educational levels

44. Hierarchy in business relationships

45. How time is understood and used

46. Whether schedules are important

47. How important tradition and rituals are

48. How often we smile, to whom we smile, and what it means when we smile

49. How strangers interact

50. How we interact with authority

51. How we interact with a person serving us, such as in a restaurant

52. Relationships and obligations between friends

53. Relationships and obligations toward family members and relatives

54. Facial expressions, gestures—when we use them

55. How we behave in a crowd or audience

56. How important preparing for the future is

57. How we see old age and value elders

58. Whether conversation should be formal or informal

59. What should be said or left unsaid

60. Whether, when, how, and with whom we make small talk

61. What we see as friendly or unfriendly

62. How open we are with information

63. What is ethical and what is not

64. How, with whom, and how much we entertain

65. How or whether we take turns or stand in line

66. How often we move and why

And much, much more!

> **Manager Tip:** When you do not see eye to eye with someone else, ask yourself which differences on this list might tell you why.

HOW DO DIFFERENCES AFFECT WORK?

The list of "66 Ways People Differ" gives a bigger picture of people's differences. How many of these have you noticed at work? Outside of work? How many of these did you have in or around your own "box"?

Most of these differences will surface in your organization at one time or another. They help explain why some people do things differently than you do and why your organization makes certain rules.

For example, company policies may define proper behavior (#1) that you must follow every day. Different ideas about time (#45) may explain why one employee is always "on time" and why another takes deadlines less seriously. "How often we move" (#66) may explain why one employee looks forward to relocation while another would rather lose a good job than move to a new town.

These 66 differences, and many more, come up in meetings, policies, work events, presentations–just about anywhere. Pick five of the 66 and tell how they show up where you work.

1. #_____affects my workplace by _____

2. #_____affects my workplace by _____

3. #_____affects my workplace by _____

4. #_____affects my workplace by _____

5. #_____affects my workplace by _____

Return to the 66 list from time to time. It will help you see and respect others' differences. It will suggest ways that you and your organization can act and shape policies to fit the differences people bring to work with them.

Exploring Your Values

Knowing your own values helps you see why and how you do certain things. On each line below, place an X on the line between the values in A and B to show which values you feel closer to.

A		**B**
I like to be doing things.	—┼—┼—┼—┼—	I like to take time to just think about things.
I like newness and change.	—┼—┼—┼—┼—	I prefer tradition and fixed rules.
I am casual and informal.	—┼—┼—┼—┼—	I am official and formal.
When I work for my own benefit, the company benefits.	—┼—┼—┼—┼—	When I work for the good of the company, I benefit too.
I like my privacy.	—┼—┼—┼—┼—	I am open and have no secrets.
I believe in equality.	—┼—┼—┼—┼—	Some people are more important than others.
I like to compete.	—┼—┼—┼—┼—	I like to cooperate.
I like quick, fast results.	—┼—┼—┼—┼—	I like results that come from long, hard work.
I like plans and structure.	—┼—┼—┼—┼—	I like things to remain flexible.
I live to work.	—┼—┼—┼—┼—	I work to live.
I tend to use clear, simple language.	—┼—┼—┼—┼—	I tend to use lots of words and try to cover all the angles.
I question authority.	—┼—┼—┼—┼—	I respect authority.

Manager Tip: How might your employees see themselves if they did this exercise? You might use it as an icebreaker at the start of a meeting. Ask people to mark where they turn up on the chart and then share some of their results. This will help you understand your workforce better and will give them a good team-building experience.

How Values Affect Behavior

Your range of values comes from your background and personal preferences. They affect what you do and how you do it. Can you identify how? Pick three values from the A and/or B lists and describe one way that each influences you.

Example: *Because I am official and formal, I tend to use people's family names and titles when addressing them, such as Mrs. Ramirez or Dr. Hintz.*

1. Because I_____, I tend to_____

_____

2. Because I_____, I tend to_____

_____

3. Because I_____, I tend to_____

_____

Outsiders often use the items in Column A in the exercise to describe American culture. How well do you fit this generalization?

Describing a group of people in general terms leads to stereotypes, which are oversimplified generalizations. Just as you may not identify yourself with each and every "American" value on the list, you cannot assume that others will fit your stereotype of their group.

Considering Differing Values

A person whose values differ from yours will do things differently from you. Pick one of the preceding values that you feel strongly about, and think what it would be like to hold its opposite.

Example: My Value: *I am official and formal.*

Someone who is casual and informal might talk the same way to everyone no matter what the person's position. Thus, such a person might see me as stiff or old-fashioned. I might think that more casual people are disrespectful when they do not call me by my title.

My Value:

_____

Someone who values the opposite might:

_____

This person would probably see me as:

_____

In turn, I might think of someone who valued the opposite as being:

_____

Rethinking Your Biases and Assumptions

Imagine it is your first day on a new job. You struggle to sort out the new from the familiar so you can adjust to your new workplace. You would be overwhelmed if *everything* was new about your job, so you expect certain things to be the same. You assume your desk and phone will work like other desks and phones you have used. You expect that your new company will have certain rules and expectations similar to ones you have experienced in the past.

Our minds expect the same when we meet new people. We assume things about how they will be. We look for traits we are familiar with. When we meet a man, we expect him to act differently from a woman. This process is natural and we need it to make sense of the world. Usually we do not even notice it.

Diversity asks you to go off "automatic pilot" and look at the assumptions you carry around. Because off-target assumptions affect how we treat other people, we face the uncomfortable but necessary challenge of changing how we think.

Let's See How This Works...

Finish the following sentences with the first thing that comes to mind:

Men...

Young people today...

Asians...

Salespeople...

Lesbians...

White people...

Politicians...

Muslims...

Native Americans...

People with disabilities...

What you hear or see is your mind's automatic way of thinking about each of these groups. Did any of your assumptions surprise you?

Avoiding the Risks in Autopilot Thinking

Although making assumptions is normal, running on autopilot carries three risks:

➤ Your assumptions may not be rooted in fact–but in false information

➤ You may treat an assumption as truth, rather than just as a possibility

➤ Unchecked assumptions say more about you than about the group you are thinking about

An assumption can be correct, partly correct, or not true at all. Make it a habit to check out your assumptions. If you do not know where an assumption came from, or it is based on only a few sources, get more information and rethink it by applying the guidelines that follow:

➤ **Treat your assumptions as possibilities, not certainties**

Most of us do not like to be wrong, nor do we like to work more than we have to, so we often tell ourselves that certain people or actions support our assumptions when they really do not. This is called a *confirmation bias*. Assumptions are just possibilities, or best guesses. They are not guaranteed to fit each person you deal with. To get off autopilot, *make it a habit to look for ways that the person does not fit your ideas*. You will soon start paying attention to more of these differences.

➤ **Make sure your assumptions aren't defensive**

Coming face-to-face with unfamiliar situations and people, it is natural to be on guard because we do not know what to expect or may not know how to act. It is easy to build assumptions based on fear, perhaps remembering warnings or bad things others have told us. Groups different from our own start to look wrong, dangerous, or inferior to us. Then we side with "our own" and do not "get" these other groups. It is called *prejudice* because we *prejudge* others without real data.

How can you identify a prejudice? When you say something about another person or group, try to sense how much feeling or emotion is stored in what you say. If there is a lot, there is a big chance that you are not being fair or accurate.

CHECKING YOUR ASSUMPTIONS: THE FAIRNESS TEST

Do this exercise privately. In the left-hand column below, list five types of people in your organization, such as work-related groups (departments, job types, learning styles) or general groups (ethnicity, gender, age). For each "type" you listed, write down in the right-hand column how your mind's "autopilot" describes these people.

_____   _____

_____   _____

_____   _____

_____   _____

_____   _____

Pick one or more of the groups you listed, then ask yourself the questions in this checklist about the assumptions you make about them.

✔ Where does my assumption come from? Is it based on what I have heard in the media, other people's stories, or generalizations from rumors?

✔ Do I have enough information to rely on it?

✔ What do I need to do to get accurate information?

✔ How is this person or situation different from what I would expect?

✔ Is my assumption emotionally loaded? Is it colored by my fear, defensiveness, or discomfort with people who are different from me?

✔ Does my assumption say more about me than about them?

✔ Am I treating these people a certain way because of my assumptions or because I have gotten to know them?

From your answers, list any assumptions that do not pass the fairness test—that lack information or are clouded by emotions. Commit yourself to reexamine them.

_____

_____

_____

Make it a habit to think outside the box when you address your biases. Look for missing information and facts you may be ignoring. Ask what about *you* causes you to make this assumption.

Learning About Others

If your assumptions need attention, you will need information that helps you to evaluate or change them. For information about other cultures and groups of people:

➤ Get to know people from different backgrounds. Keep your questions objective such as, "Tell me about the food people in your culture eat," rather than, "Why do you eat such weird stuff?" The trick is to see things as they see them, rather than making them wrong or strange because they are different.

➤ Immerse yourself in another culture by going to a meeting, gathering, or event that is important to that group. Ask a person from that culture to go with you and explain things to you.

➤ Get facts about the values, traditions, and history of other groups by reading books, articles, and Web sites.

➤ Look for special radio stations, newspapers, and TV shows that cater to other groups and tell about their concerns and interests.

On the Internet, you have all this at your fingertips. You can chat online with people from different countries and safely ask questions that you may have been reluctant to ask in person. You can go to culture-specific sites and read about the history and habits of these groups.

Manager Tip: Share the resources you find with your employees. Build an online library of information and resources so your employees can educate themselves.[5]

---

[5] An excellent resource is the *DIVERSOPHY*® game, which can be found at www.diversophy.com.

Exploring Diversity Through Your Interests

Learning about different groups is more fun if you connect it to things you already enjoy doing. If you like to watch sports, learn about other cultures' favorite sports. If you like to chat online, join chat groups made up of different kinds of people. Tell them that you are interested in getting new perspectives. What are the issues of gay parents? What is family life like in the military? If you like to cook, learn how to make Chinese New Year's dumplings. If you like festivities, celebrate *El día de los muertos* and St. Patrick's Day with the local Latino or Irish community. Bring intercultural dimensions to social events and activities at your workplace.

When you attend events from different cultures, try to understand activities and perspectives different from your own. Be conscious of negative judgments based on ethnocentrism on your part.

Think about three things you like, and then note how you can make them more fun by adding diversity to them:

Activity: **I can add diversity by:**

1. _____   _____

   _____

2. _____   _____

   _____

3. _____   _____

   _____

Becoming a Diversity Leader

As a manager you have a special responsibility toward diversity. Not only must you develop yourself to handle the many diverse situations that occur in the workplace, you also are called upon to be a *diversity leader*—to help create a climate that values diversity, fairness, and inclusion.

The values and behavior of your organization, whether it works face-to-face or online, depends on what people do or say to create positive or negative feelings. Respecting diversity and supporting people in their differences, in both crises and day-to-day activity, create a culture where all people feel valued and appreciated.

Don't Fall into the Law Trap

Some managers find it hard to separate diversity from the laws made to protect it. They focus only on making sure they are following policies and are within the law. Do not get caught in this trap. Keeping the law is important but only a starting point. Do not stop there. Diversity would be a positive and useful mind-set and way of doing business even if there were no laws about it.

If you spend little time learning about the possibilities that differences bring and helping people take advantage of their differences, you cannot be a diversity leader. How you lead and behave toward others has more power and influence than policies and regulations.

See the law as a necessary fallback position but not as a substitute for your own sense of fairness and your ability to include and get the best out of others. Many dimensions of diversity are not included in the law but must be considered to create an inclusive workplace that benefits from the resources that differences bring. Laws cannot generate creativity and commitment in managing diversity. You can.

> **Manager Tip:** Laws ensure people are treated fairly at work. But it is your *leadership,* not laws and regulations, that enables your employees to work together successfully.

Making Diversity Your C-H-O-I-C-E

An active diversity mind-set can be summed up in the word *CHOICE,* which stands for the six key elements. They are:

C ommitment

H onesty

O penness

I nclusiveness

C reativity

E xplicitness

Be **Committed** to making diversity succeed.

Be **Honest** with yourself. Analyze your assumptions. Tell others about your feelings and intentions. Admit when you make a mistake.

Be **Open** to new ways of doing things and other ways of thinking.

Be **Inclusive** in your language, policies, and events. Make sure all employees know that they belong and are valued.

Be **Creative** in how you approach situations, give presentations, and solve problems. Step outside the box to address and profit from people's different styles and needs.

Be **Explicit** in your words and intentions and do so in a respectful way, to avoid misunderstanding. Say what you mean and clarify what you meant if you are misunderstood.

Make it your *choice* to support diversity. Use these principles to guide your decisions and actions.

> Leading diversity means taking active steps to ensure that your organization develops with you in becoming more diversity-competent.

Getting IN-IN-IN to the Diversity Mind-set

Comfort with different cultures, backgrounds, and lifestyles comes more easily if you can appreciate what they have to offer. IN-IN-IN is a way to think about diversity and unfamiliar situations. IN-IN-IN stands for three habits that diversity teaches: *Interest, Introspection,* and *Innovation.* Let's look at each of these individually.

INterest

How would your life be different if you had grown up in someone else's shoes? What would it be like to work in a different department, to have a co-worker's job, or to coordinate your work schedule with four children's after-school activities? Interacting with people whose lives and duties differ from your own gives you a chance to learn a lot about your organization and society—as well as yourself.

When you meet those different from you, ask what makes them special and take time to get to know what their lives are like. Be curious. Start to see the subtle differences that make the world more colorful and intriguing. It is okay to ask why people do what they do. Even they may not always know the answer, but you will enjoy some rich and interesting conversations.

INtrospection

You may not have a good picture of your own beliefs and actions until you come across something that jars your thinking. You catch yourself disagreeing with someone before you suddenly realize what you really believe and why. Similarly, you may not realize you have an aversion to eating with your hands or asking favors for friends until you find yourself giving a dirty look to someone doing just that. Diversity teaches us about ourselves.

INnovation

Diverse outlooks create some of the most powerful and innovative ideas. The saying "two heads are better than one" stems from the idea that each person has something to offer that will create a better result. Bounce your thoughts off other people to create a more well-rounded idea.

Opportunities to innovate occur daily in the workplace. When thinking through a new idea, get feedback from someone who thinks differently from you. How can you shape a good sexual harassment policy if you do not talk with people of the opposite sex and of different sexual orientations about their different needs and experiences?

Because some people look at the big picture while others are more concerned with the details, they can help you catch loopholes that your thinking style might miss.

When differences show up in others, think of them as opportunities rather than threats. You can better face what is new or foreign to you if you use the IN-IN-IN approach.

CHECK YOUR OWN MIND-SET

The IN-IN-IN approach can help you find your core differences so you can use them to become more open to diversity. Begin by describing a recent time when you found yourself in an uncomfortable situation with someone:

_____

_____

_____

_____

Now ask yourself these IN-IN-IN questions:

1. INterest questions:

What differences could have been contributing to this situation?

_____

_____

What do I know or could I ask about these differences?

_____

_____

2. INtrospection questions:

Why did I call these things "differences" in the first place? What is it about mc that makes this a difference?

_____

_____

What did I learn about myself from this experience?

_____

_____

How do I react when I come across a difference like this?

_____

_____

_____

CONTINUED

3. INnovation questions:

How did our differences affect what we saw and felt?

_____

_____

What can this person teach me to help me improve my ideas? What can I offer to this person?

_____

_____

How might understanding and using our differences have helped us to reach a better understanding?

_____

_____

HOW DO YOU FEEL ABOUT EMBRACING DIVERSITY?

Diversity challenges you to change how you think and act. Everyone has different levels of tolerance for change. The more change scares you, the harder it is to value diversity and make the changes needed to work with it.

Check your comfort level for change on the following diagrams. Circle the statement that best fits how you feel about diversity.

Becoming more diverse will bring positive changes to my organization.

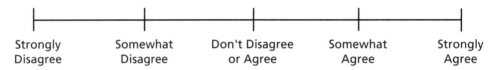

| Strongly Disagree | Somewhat Disagree | Don't Disagree or Agree | Somewhat Agree | Strongly Agree |

I feel energized and ready to start taking a leading role on diversity challenges.

| Strongly Disagree | Somewhat Disagree | Don't Disagree or Agree | Somewhat Agree | Strongly Agree |

This is a change I think I can handle.

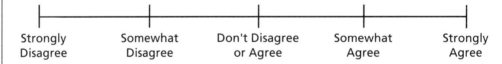

| Strongly Disagree | Somewhat Disagree | Don't Disagree or Agree | Somewhat Agree | Strongly Agree |

I realize I'll make some mistakes along the way, and that's okay.

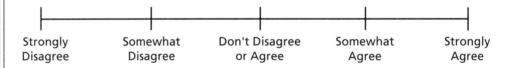

| Strongly Disagree | Somewhat Disagree | Don't Disagree or Agree | Somewhat Agree | Strongly Agree |

I am comfortable asking for help from people different from myself.

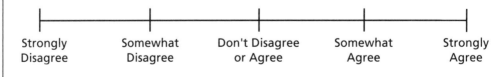

| Strongly Disagree | Somewhat Disagree | Don't Disagree or Agree | Somewhat Agree | Strongly Agree |

Transitioning Through Change

If the exercise you just completed uncovered some uncertainty in you about embracing diversity, realize that it is normal to be anxious about change. In fact, there are four common stages of what is called *diversity shock*. You and the people you work with are likely to go through the following stages again and again:

Stage 1: You love it. New people are interesting and different. If you are one of them, the new environment is fresh and challenging.

Stage 2: You hate it. You don't know how to deal with the "others," the local culture, the unwritten rules.

Stage 3: You learn to live with it. You start learning what works, start asking hard questions, and take others as they are without trying to change them.

Stage 4: You make something out of it. You discover new possibilities in others and in yourself that make your work together more productive and interesting.

Embracing Change with Confidence

Consider the following points about change and apply these tips to boost your confidence as you work through the stages of diversity shock:

➤ Knowing the **value** of changing the way you do something will motivate you to get started. Remind yourself of the value of diversity. Think *Interest, Introspection, Innovation*. What's in it for you?

➤ Change requires **energy** but not as much as you may fear. Tell other supportive people about your dedication to diversity. Sharing your excitement will give you the energy to make things happen.

➤ If you know you do not have to change everything overnight, you will feel more in **control**. Start small. Each little step you take will give you more energy for the next one.

➤ Change creates **room for mistakes** because everything is new. Mistakes are a healthy part of learning; they help you learn what not to do in the future. No one expects you to get everything right from the beginning, so do not let a fear of mistakes keep you from starting.

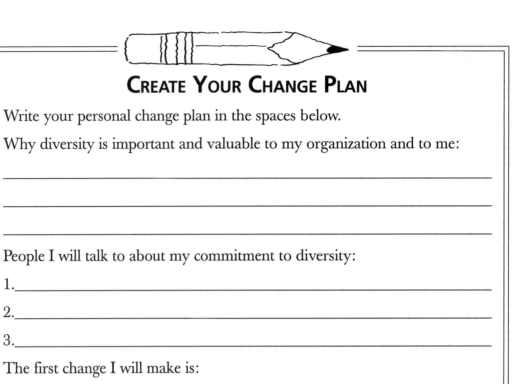

CREATE YOUR CHANGE PLAN

Write your personal change plan in the spaces below.

Why diversity is important and valuable to my organization and to me:

_____

_____

_____

People I will talk to about my commitment to diversity:

1._____

2._____

3._____

The first change I will make is:

_____

The first mistake I will probably make is:

_____

Manager Tip: When proposing changes in your organization, make sure the value of the change to your employees is clear to them. Let them know it is okay to make mistakes along the way.

Progress Check

The first page of Part 2 informed you that the following statements were all false. Can you now explain why? Hint: Think about the lessons you have just learned to help you in disproving these statements.

❏ *"Diversity is really about women and minorities."*

_____

_____

❏ *"Diversity training is just another passing business trend."*

_____

_____

❏ *"I'm not prejudiced."*

_____

_____

❏ *"Diversity concerns Human Resources, not line managers."*

_____

_____

❏ *"The best way to deal with diversity is to just follow laws and policies."*

_____

_____

❏ *"Just treat everyone the same and there will be no problem."*

_____

_____

❏ *"Talking about diversity only separates us further."*

_____

_____

Compare your answers to the authors' suggested responses in the Appendix.

_____

To work more on your personal development in the area of diversity, read *Working Together: Succeeding in a Multicultural Organization,* also by George Simons, Crisp Publications, 2003.

Leading and Communicating

“If we seek to understand a people, we have to try to put ourselves, as far as we can, in their particular historical and cultural backgrounds. We have to use their language, not language in the narrow sense, but the language of the mind.”

—Jawaharlal Nehru, First Prime Minister of India

50

Outlining Diversity Competencies for Managers

The following checklist outlines diversity competencies a manager must have to lead effectively. Some were covered in Part 2 and the rest are addressed in the remainder of this book. How able do you feel in each area? Check (✔) your ability level for each competence in the right-hand columns.

Personal Qualities	Easy for me	Need help
1. I can recognize my own biases and assumptions about others.		
2. I recognize there is more than one way to lead or be successful, and I can include different styles and cultures in decision-making, brainstorming, and feedback meetings. I know how to use what others have to offer.		
3. I can get objective information about the cultures of employees and external customers. This includes history, values, holidays, and so on.		
4. I can relate diversity to the business case and overall business strategy.		
5. I can listen objectively to complaints about harassment, inappropriate remarks, and behavior.		
6. I can describe how various markets (ethnic, gender, sexual orientation) affect our business.		
7. I am comfortable with different cultures.		
8. I know the laws related to disability, race, gender, and religion.		
9. I can hold people accountable for the quality of their work, whatever their background or culture.		
10. I am familiar with the different kinds of diversity and can speak comfortably about them with others.		

CONTINUED

Leadership Skills	Easy for me	Need help
11. I can speak and present clearly to a diverse audience.		
12. I can create solid relationships with people who think and act differently from me.		
13. I know how to listen to, influence, and motivate diverse individuals and groups.		
14. I am prepared to mentor, coach, and develop the people under me, whatever their background.		
15. I can use organizational "street sense" and know where and how to get things done in the organization.		
16. I can model and encourage open communication and effective teamwork.		
17. I know how to and am willing to manage conflicts, disagreements, and claims of harassment.		

CONTINUED

Personnel Management and Performance Evaluation	Easy for me	Need help
18. I am clear about the basic qualifications and competencies that are needed to fill a position.		
19. I can conduct target interviews and not allow assumptions and biases to influence my decisions— for example, hiring someone just because he is from the same culture or gender or because she is from a particular ethnic or racial background.		
20. I can apply the laws about the questions that are appropriate to ask in an interview and those that are not.		
21. I can measure an employee's diversity competencies in an evaluation.		
22. I am comfortable in giving evaluations based on performance.		
23. I can document critical diversity incidents.		
24. I am able to find out what motivates different kinds of people to do their best work and what hinders them.		
25. I know how to study best practices of other organizations and transfer them to my own group.		
26. I know how to develop a large candidate pool for hiring and promotions.		
27. I can create effective measurements of diversity success in hiring, retention, and managing complaints.		
28. I know how to hire a good diversity consultant.		

Communicating Face-to-Face

Many books seek to help you improve your basic communication skills. This one focuses on tools that are particularly useful when diversity is likely to be a critical factor in communicating with others.

It has been rightly observed that when groups are diverse, "common sense isn't common anymore." It takes extra work to create understanding and find direction, but our decisions and our creativity are often much richer for having made the effort. So not surprisingly, listening and questioning come before speaking and influencing when dealing with diverse groups.

Cultural Differences

Face-to-face meetings are highly important for building trust, and some cultural groups rely on them more than others. The diagram below shows, generally, the importance of face-to-face relationship building—from highly important to less important—in various cultural groups around the world:

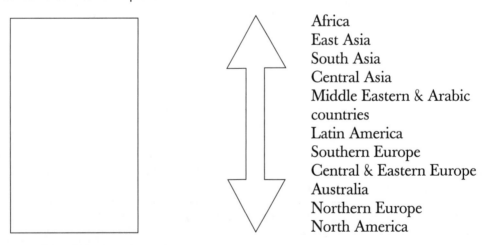

Face-to-face **more** important

Africa
East Asia
South Asia
Central Asia
Middle Eastern & Arabic countries
Latin America
Southern Europe
Central & Eastern Europe
Australia
Northern Europe
North America

Face-to-face **less** important

Of course, individuals within any culture may differ, and people who have become accustomed to living in another culture may "double code." That is, sometimes they behave like the culture they are living in, and sometimes (usually when stress is high or the issue is important) they revert to the values of their root culture.

Gauging People You Know

Think about people from diverse backgrounds that you usually work with. In the box to the left of the arrow, jot down their names. Where would you put them on this scale? Does their position on the scale tell you something about how you may have missed important signals in the past or how you may better relate to them in the future?

Asking Questions to Create Rapport

Sharing how we interpret and respond to what goes on between and around us is a key piece of creating rapport and common values. Asking good questions can help a diverse group discuss how individual members view and react to the same event or experience.

These discussion questions generally fall into the four categories outlined below.[6] As you ask the questions, make sure you hear what everyone has to say, not just the most vocal group members.

Sense

These questions draw out the facts about an experience or event and help us recall information and details. Sample questions:

➤ What did you see?

➤ Who was there?

➤ What scenes do you remember?

➤ What words or phrases caught your attention?

➤ What were some of the key actions you saw?

Feel

What feelings did people have about an event or experience? These questions bring feelings out into the open. Sample questions:

➤ When or where were you surprised? intrigued? angered? pleased? frustrated? amused?

➤ What was your first reaction?

➤ Do you remember others reacting? When? How?

---

[6]Adapted from "Tools for Creating Positive Dialogue–The Top© Conversation Method," by Gae Broadwater, in *Faces of Diversity,* National Center for Diversity, Kentucky State University, April 1997, page 3. The Top© Focused Conversation Method is presented in *Winning Through Participation: Meeting the Challenge of Corporate Change with the Technology of Participation,* by Laura Spencer, Kendall-Hunt Publishing, 1996.

Interpret

What meaning or value are people placing on the event or experience? What do they see as its significance and impact on the group or project? Sample questions:

➤ What is this about?

➤ Where have you experienced something like this?

➤ Why is this important?

➤ Which of these would be a first priority?

➤ What trends do you see emerging?

➤ What connections do you make to our current procedures?

Decide and Act

These questions help the group to determine what action it should take. Sample questions:

➤ What do you or we need to do?

➤ What story would you tell about this?

➤ What are the implications of this for us?

➤ What is the resolve of this group?

Facilitating discussions with these questions enables you to avoid misunderstandings that happen when people talk on different levels, such as one person telling how he felt while another is asking for action.

When you experience a cultural conflict with a co-worker, you can also ask yourself the following questions:

➤ What do I actually see and hear?

➤ What feelings do I have about it?

➤ How do I interpret the event?

Increasing Employee Involvement

No organization wants to pay people for not performing to their fullest potential. Yet many organizations and managers do just that by not knowing how to put diversity to work. This section looks at ways you can increase the input and creativity you get from your diverse employees.

A. Think of how you make decisions and whom you listen to on your team. Write down your decision-making process.

> What are the steps I take to come to a decision?

B. List the names of the people you listen to the most in the left-hand column below.

1.	
2.	
3.	

C. In the left-hand column below, write the names of people from whom you do not solicit ideas or who are not likely to offer ideas to you.

1.	
2.	
3.	

Is it the same few people each time who have the most input and credibility with you?

Now go back to the first list (the people you listen to the most) and, in the right-hand column next to each name, write each person's personality characteristics and cultural, racial, and ethnic background, and what you like about the individual.

Do the same thing for the people you do not listen to as much. List their personality characteristics, why you do not listen to them, and anything you do not like about them.

Review each list and circle the commonalities of the people you listen to, and then circle the commonalities of those you do not listen to. Are there any patterns? Do you find that you get input from one type of person, such as the extroverts who offer their thoughts without always having to be asked, or that you are more comfortable talking with people from your age group or religious affiliation?

After you have done this exercise, pick out one or two people with whom you have not talked very much and ask for their input on a project you are involved with or ideas for new projects. At first these people might be reticent, but if they see that you are seriously interested in them, you might be surprised at their feedback or new ideas.

Studies have shown that heterogeneous teams (where people are different) solve problems more creatively than homogeneous teams (where people are the same). For that to happen, however, the teams must be functional where everyone is encouraged and allowed to contribute.

Ten Tips for Managing Multicultural Employees[7]

1. **Lay out clear lines of communication, organizational structure, and tasks.** Avoid instituting change for change's sake, because the people you are managing may see this as unstable and unreliable, rather than innovative.

2. **Set recognizable milestones for performance.** To avoid creating confusion and false assumptions, managers of culturally diverse employees must set clear and quantifiable expectations for all employees.

3. **Avoid assigning roles to people based on stereotypes.** Assuming that people are "good with numbers" or "creative types" because of national or ethnic origin can underuse individual talents.

4. **Be careful about how you promote people from performance alone.** Seniority structures and family ties may be strong, and promotions "out of line" may offend other employees.

5. **Keep in constant touch to reinforce progress and identify problems.** In many settings, it is the manager's responsibility to recognize when an employee is dissatisfied or troubled.

6. **Invest in training.** Studies have shown that diverse teams that learn together perform better.

7. **Avoid overanalyzing problems and concentrate on what is working.** An overly analytical style can seem critical or argumentative in some cultural settings.

8. **Form a network of cultural mentors.** Find "cultural mentors" that can help you distinguish between personal, organizational, and cultural issues.

9. **Set a realistic pace to meet goals.** Tasks and projects across national boundaries and with people of different languages or cultural orientations always take longer.

10. **Build similarities by recognizing differences.** Try to find out about issues and concerns *before* creating policies and procedures.

---

[7] These tips are provided by Marcella Simon Peralta of Peralta Associates, http://peraltaassociates.com.

Putting Diversity to Work Electronically

Most management and diversity training assumes that people almost always work face-to-face. In fact, today most people in most organizations are working *virtually* with one another most of the time.

Having top management champion an organization's diversity effort is still the No. 1 key to success. But *online support* is coming up fast among the best practices that keep a diversity initiative humming. This is not surprising because in many organizations today, much more communication happens online via e-mail and chat, and by phone and teleconference, than occurs face-to-face. In fact, in some organizations the amount of communication that takes place via e-mail, the Internet, telephone, teleconferencing, videoconferencing, and so on—as opposed to meeting face-to-face—approaches 90%.

How much of your communication is done at a distance? Use the space below to draw a map showing where the people are that you work with regularly. Circle those people with whom you cooperate most of the time without seeing them face-to-face. Check (✔) the ones who come from different cultures or backgrounds. Then estimate what percentage of your communication with them is by electronic media.

Showing Your Organization's Diversity Online

Does the (inter)face that your organization shows online truly show its diversity and tell how the company values diversity and benefits from it?

The following is a checklist of diversity principles for online platforms. The list starts with your online team room and reaches all the way up to the company's public Web site. If you are thinking of or starting to build such a platform, keep these principles in mind. If you already have a site, bring it up on your computer screen and look at it as you check through this list.

❑ Does the site tell you about the organization's diversity and its commitment to valuing diversity in its daily operations?

❑ Is diversity of your people obvious from the images used? Do both images and text carry cultural messages that are accurate and appropriate for the site's end users?

❑ Does the site meet the cultural and linguistic needs of all its users? (This is called *globalization and localization*.). If English is the only language used, is plain and clear language the rule?

❑ Is there diversity-related information about the group or company on the home page or not more than one click away?

❑ Is the site indexed so that you get results when you search for the keyword "diversity" or other common diversity topics?

❑ Is the diversity information on the site updated regularly?

Let's look in more detail at how Web sites, especially the three most common kinds—intranets, extranets, and the Internet itself—can help you spread your diversity effort and get others to support it.

The Company Intranet

An *intranet* is an online corporate work space usually reserved for those on the company network. It is where you store and deliver the organization's or the group's information, discuss and develop work plans, offer e-learning, and maybe even have space for socializing. In short, depending on what your organization produces, it may be anything from a set of tools to the place where the company does most of what it does. Many companies today create, develop, market, and sell their products or services exclusively online.

Even if your company is not one of these, the company intranet is as much a diverse workplace as the actual bricks-and-mortar buildings that make up offices, factories, and other workplaces. Managing diversity and supporting diversity efforts online is not any less important than on the shop floor. Check it out:

❑ Are employee affinity groups given space on the site and encouraged to use it? (An affinity group is a group formed within a company to represent the interests of a specific diverse group within the organization, such as the black managers' caucus, gay-lesbian alliance, and the like.)

❑ Are diversity events publicized?

❑ Is there e-learning that supports corporate training in diversity?

❑ Is online learning and information adapted to people's different learning and work styles?

❑ Is the online work space so designed that disabled employees can effectively use it?

The Extranet

An *extranet* is a secure or protected online site that serves those company functions that involve outsiders, such as a supplier or distributor networks or outsourced operations. Here the company shows itself to and interacts with other key individuals and organizations, so it must make sure that its diversity values are loud and clear, including what it expects in diversity behavior from the organizations it works with. Business-to-business e-commerce is quickly replacing more traditional methods of sourcing material and personnel. Check it out:

❏ Is their a clear plan and strategy for developing the extranet as a diversity showcase for the company's values and initiatives?

❏ Does the site make clear the company policies and values that affect suppliers and partners who deal with the company?

❏ Does the site encourage supplier diversity?

❏ Are the interface, navigation aids, and help desk adapted to the needs and thinking of diverse end users?

The Internet

The *Internet* is where the organization meets the world. A company Web site may serve as a brochure, the company newsletter, and the financial report to stakeholders and stockholders. It may be a place for marketing, sales, recruiting, e-commerce, and many more functions. It is where people who want to work or do business with you are likely to see you first—without your even knowing it—before they even think of visiting or speaking to you. Such a site offers countless opportunities to show diversity leadership. Check it out:

❏ Is there a clear plan and strategy for developing the corporate Web site as a diversity showcase for the company's values and initiatives?

❏ Are the organization's commitment to diversity and its business goals clear in the mission and values statements, the CEO's welcome, and other statements?

❏ Does the site offer diversity information in its career or recruitment areas? Does it picture diverse people in management positions?

❏ Does the site highlight company activities that affect diverse markets and respond to the needs of diverse communities?

❏ Are the company's internal and external diversity efforts and successes evident?

Leading and Managing Diversity Online

Working at a distance has both pluses and minuses for diversity. When we are working side-by-side, the ways people behave and look may trigger our biases or just get under our skin. But we do not see these anymore when we work via e-mail and the Internet, and so we may ignore these differences.

On the minus side, this means we often miss the clues we would usually see when working face-to-face. So we do not know what is going on in the background among the people we are working with. Sometimes lack of trust and uncomfortable feelings become big blocks to online teamwork. We fail to see them until it is too late to fix them.

The following are the basic rules for leading and managing diversity online:

> **Culture is working whether we see it or not.** People on the other end of the discussion continue to see things in their own time frame, with their own ideas and values and their own decision-making.

> **Creating and maintaining trust** is the biggest responsibility of leading a diverse virtual team. You make trust possible and keep it alive when:

  - You do what you say you are going to do. You make promises and keep them.

  - You tell others about your values and you live by them. Everyone you work with should know what you stand for. They have a right to expect fairness, respect, and integrity, even though in a diverse group we may have to learn how these may be expressed in different ways.

  - You are competent in doing your job. Performance is an important trust factor. You should know what you are doing and how to do it, and be ready to learn what you do not know or what you could do better.

  - You respect cultural differences and discuss them. When people differ about how they see and respond to an issue, talk about it rather than avoiding it. Get agreement on whose approach or what mix of approaches to take.

  - You *care about* and *care for* the people you work with. This is the most powerful trust builder. Caring may involve friendship, but it does not have to. It is the habit of acting in people's best interest and supporting them personally. People trust you when they know that you want them to succeed in their organizational and personal lives.

➤ **Reflecting on how we work together is as much a part of the job as getting the task done.** Diverse teams must discuss differences in how they think and perform, whether they work face-to-face or online. It takes extra effort to manage and do this at a distance.

➤ **Virtual teams and workers must agree on the right media to use, when, and with whom.** All our electronic tools have their pluses and minuses. We want to choose and use them to meet the needs of diverse workers and teams. The tips in the next section can help you decide how to use the most common media.

Using Electronic Tools Effectively

New ways of working are now commonplace, but understanding and using the new virtual workplace well is not easy, especially when processes and technology change rapidly. Implement the following tips and create the standards that work best for everyone in your group for collaborating across time, space, and culture.

E-Mail [8]

E-mail is the most commonly—and most inefficiently—used element in the virtual toolbox. Someone once said, "If all you have is a hammer, everything looks like a nail." People use e-mail for everything—often badly. The following table—and the 10 tips page that follows this section—outline how to use e-mail more effectively.

Possibilities	Challenges	Solutions
Because e-mail lets you read and respond at your own pace, it is useful for people who like to work on several tasks at once, especially when they work with people who like to do one thing at a time.	Delays in answering e-mails might indicate team problems, such as low trust, concrete problems with the project, or cultural differences, such as people's different notions of time.	Set team norms for when and how you will use e-mail, who gets copies, how long messages should be, how soon to respond, and how formally people should be addressed.
Group-oriented people may find that e-mail is a good means to exchange information after trust has been built.	Short and informal e-mails that sound friendly to some may sound short, rude, angry, or impersonal to others. Some people discuss things openly that others think should be confidential. Those who are working in a second language and worry about spelling and grammar might be hesitant to respond if language seems too difficult.	To send important or confidential messages or resolve conflicts, use a more personal approach, a telephone call, or if possible a face-to-face meeting.
If people speak different languages, e-mail gives time to use translation services, dictionaries, and other tools.		Avoid slang. Use simple, correct English. Use multimedia e-mail or other media that meet diverse learning and working styles. Team members can offer to edit texts for second-language users.

[8]These tips are part of a larger set developed by a virtual team composed of Assumpta Aneas, Spain: aaneas@d5.ub.es; Catherine Cosgrove, Canada: catherine.cosgrove@clarica.com; Anna Shirley Harper, Australia: aharp@ozemail.com.au; Anne Niesen, Germany: info@aniesen.de; Emily Reich, United States: emily@groupjazz.com; and George Simons, France: gsimons@diversophy.com.

Online Work Spaces

Online discussion forums, bulletin boards, calendars, task lists, and the like are examples of online work spaces that can help us set goals and plans, topics and tasks that a team faces. But just like e-mail, these electronic media have their pitfalls. The following table sorts out the pros and cons.

Possibilities	Challenges	Solutions
Online work spaces let everyone see what is going on. They allow people to join and work at their own pace in the order that works best for them.	People can easily fall behind if they cannot participate as much as other team members because of language problems, disabilities, or differences in technology and varying levels of online skills	Make sure that everyone has access to the workplace and that people get to know each other. Pay attention to the pace of the discussion and encourage less outgoing participants to regularly take part in the discussion.
Work spaces are more complex and richer than e-mail. They pay off handsomely when leaders take time to create and facilitate them toward specific deadlines.	People easily fall back on old favorite tools like excessive e-mail memos and long phone chats, according to their cultural preferences. Some are embarrassed to ask for help if they are stuck.	Educate everyone to access and use these tools. Pay attention to the impact of different tools on different people. Facilitate actively and provide a good help desk, but also urge people to help each other.

Real-Time Media

Chat, instant messaging, teleconferencing, and videoconferencing are ways to communicate in real time, without the delays inherent in other electronic tools. But they can present challenges in a diverse workplace, as outlined in the following table.

Possibilities	Challenges	Solutions
Chat can help build emotional bridges and trust between team members and give a stronger sense of "us." It is a quick way to ask questions and clarify misunderstandings. For those who work better if they can follow several ideas at a time, chat and instant messaging can help them talk about several things at once in an unstructured, creative way.	The quick pace and shorthand style of chat may be hard for people who use a second language. Some might feel it impolite or embarrassing to ask for clarification. If an agenda has not been set in advance, the chat may be frustrating and unproductive for individualistic cultures or people with a single focus on time.	Help all participants see and respect different levels of language ability. Post explanations of common acronyms, abbreviations, and slang terms. If using charts or printed material, send copies in advance to all participants. An agenda is even more important than usual for following the discussion and preparing ideas or comments for use online.
Chats can be a quick way to connect with others and create a sense of team, particularly with more group-oriented members.	People from more individualistic and task-oriented backgrounds may think that team building by using chat and instant messaging is a waste of time.	Build in time for warmups and chitchat, but also have a firm agenda that can then move on so no one gets too frustrated.

CONTINUED

Real-Time Media, cont'd.

Possibilities	Challenges	Solutions
Teleconferencing and videoconferencing can be useful for getting parties to talk, especially if a clear agenda or advance briefing has occurred. A telephone call or teleconference can be a good middle point between e-mail and face-to-face communication, particularly when misunderstandings and conflicts arise.	Participants must be comfortable with the language being used in the telephone conference because the conversation is often rapid and there is no time to look up words. Static and delay can cause people to interrupt. There is nothing worse than sitting and listening as an outsider, feeling not included in the conversation.	Chairing a conference call is essential if all parties are to contribute and be heard. Remind participants to speak slowly and avoid slang or jargon. Choose the level of language best suited to the needs and abilities of team members. Individualistic cultures must learn to wait for a pause, reflection time, or response before jumping in. Send the agenda, charts, and important texts in advance to all teleconference participants. "Go around the room," and call on everyone for opinions.
A group videoconference or Web meeting can make a meeting into a real occasion where you are expected to be present (because you can be seen). It reinforces the sense that the group is real and interdependent.	Problems with the medium itself, as well as language concerns, may make it difficult for people to understand one another or correctly interpret facial expressions, body language, and gestures.	Have people speak more slowly than they usually would. Videoconferencing is useful at the start-up of a team to help put a face to each person, especially if a face-to-face meeting is not an option.

Ten Tips for E-Mailing Across Borders and Cultures[9]

1. **Avoid long sentences with many ideas.** Cover one question, one answer, or one announcement at a time. Try not to use too many "ands," "buts," or "ors." Use no more than 15 words per sentence.

2. **Order your ideas to help the reader.** Number or bullet segments. Use words such as "first," "next," and "last" to organize ideas into understandable sequences.

3. **Avoid vague descriptions.** Avoid using vague words such as "a few," "a lot," or "huge." Be as precise as possible: "I will be arriving in Miami on October 5 (not "soon"), and I will be staying there for five days (not "about a week").

4. **Spell out abbreviations and acronyms.** Readers may have a hard time understanding abbreviations such as FYI, ASAP, CA, HRD, or COB.

5. **Avoid idioms, slang, sarcasm, sports terminology, jargon, or doublespeak.** Most second-language speakers learn "textbook" English and may be unfamiliar with colloquial English or references to popular culture.

6. **Be careful with units of measurement.** Specify the currency, such as USD for U.S. dollars, and use metric measurements whenever needed.

7. **Remember that words may have multiple meanings.** For example, "replace" can mean "to exchange" or "to put back." Make clear the meaning you want to express by giving details or examples.

8. **Make sure phone numbers are written so they can be used internationally.** Toll-free numbers sometimes cannot be called from outside the United States. Learn and use the right country code prefixes (normally "001" for the United States and Canada) and area codes for all phone and fax numbers.

9. **Spell out the actions, and the deadlines, you want the reader to use.** "Please send me Territory 5's sales report for March 2002 no later than April 6, 2002, 5 P.M. Eastern Standard Time."

10. **Provide the reader with as much follow-up information as possible.** Include full names, titles, addresses, URLs, references, and background materials.

---

[9]These tips are provided by Marcella Simon Peralta of Peralta Associates, http://www.peraltaassociates.com

Progress Check

Part 3 has provided the basics of what a manager must know and do to succeed in a multicultural workplace and to communicate effectively.

Here are the most important action points for working on a virtual project with diverse colleagues or teams. Are they happening in your team? Do you:

- ❏ Listen to each other and discuss what you experience in this new working environment?

- ❏ Get everyone's input?

- ❏ Make sure you agree on how you will work together?

- ❏ Choose the tools you will use, and how and when you will use them?

- ❏ Decide together on common practices you will develop to handle the different sense of time, communication patterns, language, and values of your diverse colleagues?

Diversifying Your Workplace Successfully

> "*Once you can see the boundaries of your environment, they are no longer the boundaries of your environment.*"
>
> **—Marshall McLuhan, Canadian Philosopher**

Recruiting for Diversity

If you are serious about championing a diverse workforce, you must create a diverse pool of candidates. If you always recruit from the same places, you will get the same people. In a competitive market you must be creative. For example, some organizations begin recruiting in the middle schools, by sending speakers to classrooms and assemblies. Some organizations begin internship programs in high school.

Your Recruiting Strategies

Take out paper and pencil or open a new document in your word processor and list all the steps you have taken to develop and implement a diversity recruiting plan. Then ask:

➤ Is our lead time for hiring long enough to get a good selection of diverse applicants?

❑ **Yes**　　　❑ **No**　　　❑ **Don't Know**

➤ Do we have a list of schools that historically have large numbers of students of color, women, or people with disabilities, and do we try to recruit from those institutions?

❑ **Yes**　　　❑ **No**　　　❑ **Don't Know**

➤ Do we send a diverse team to meet with people at schools and other recruiting sites and build relationships so our organization will be the place of choice to apply?

❑ **Yes**　　　❑ **No**　　　❑ **Don't Know**

➤ Do we maintain contact with or support candidate pools and student groups and activities that represent diversity in race, age, sexual orientation, and so on?

❑ **Yes**　　　❑ **No**　　　❑ **Don't Know**

➤ Does our organization look welcoming, not only in how we word our recruitment pitch, but also in how diverse it looks? (That is, do we have diversity in our board of directors and at all levels of the organization so we can point to real diversity as a selling point?)

❑ **Yes**　　　❑ **No**　　　❑ **Don't Know**

➤ How is our organization viewed in the communities where we want to recruit? Do we sponsor events such as Gay Pride Week, Cinco de Mayo, Juneteenth, Chinese New Year, and other traditional celebrations and events? Do we get involved with community organizations?

❑ **Yes**　　　❑ **No**　　　❑ **Don't Know**

➤ Where have we advertised for candidates? Do we not only advertise but get interviewed in magazines such as *Hispanic, Asian Week,* and *Black Enterprise* as well as mainline economic journals?

Current places we advertise: _____

_____

New places to advertise:_____

_____

➤ Do we look for internal candidates? Can employee affinity groups help? Do we talk to suppliers and vendors that champion diversity and let them know that we have positions available? Do they have recruiting best practices we might adopt?

Affinity groups/vendors/suppliers we can talk to:_____

_____

➤ Does our Web site and promotional literature tell the world that diversity is part of our mission statement?

❑ **Yes**　　　❑ **No**　　　❑ **Don't Know**

➤ Do online photos and illustrations reflect real diversity in our organization?

❑ **Yes**　　　❑ **No**　　　❑ **Don't Know**

Now use your answers to help draft a new recruiting strategy or list steps you can take to modify or carry out an existing one with an improved diversity perspective. If you could not answer some of these questions, find people who can (usually in human resources). Invite these people to help you make diversity stand out in your recruiting strategy.

Examining Your Attitudes About Job Candidates

Despite what many believe, hiring candidates for a new position or a promotion is never completely objective. In fact, unconscious biases and assumptions always try to interfere with your ability to interview and select the best candidate. Those biases and assumptions can affect everything, including creating the candidate pool, prescreening candidates, asking interview questions, and making decisions.

Your Beliefs About Interview Behaviors

What have you been told that you still believe a candidate should *always* do in an interview?

Verbal:_____

Non-verbal:_____

What were you told and still believe that a candidate should *never* do in an interview?

Verbal:_____

Non-verbal:_____

Where did these beliefs come from?

_____

_____

Rethinking Your Beliefs

Reexamine the "should always" and "never" items you listed above and ask which ones are relevant to the positions you are hiring for and to the candidate's abilities to succeed in those jobs. Are any of these beliefs based on old stereotypes or out-of-date interviewing practices? The following examples may challenge your old beliefs:

Belief: People should always keep frequent and direct eye contact during an interview. People who do not are dishonest and disrespectful.

Fact: Many people raised in the United States hold this belief. But some Asian cultures consider it disrespectful to look directly in another person's eyes, and many African Americans' patterns of eye contact differ from those of many white people. Rather than focusing only on the eyes, look at overall body language to see if you have the interviewee's attention. If you operate on the belief that lack of eye contact is disrespectful or hides something, you will not really believe what the applicant says.

Belief: A man should never wear a beard for an interview.

Fact: Facial hair does not affect a person's ability to do a job. Even in the food service industry where it is important to keep hair away from food, men can cover their beards with nets. Sometimes sporting facial hair is in keeping with religious beliefs.

Belief: Clothing styles and fashions, piercings and tattoos, speech styles and accents, and personal care tell a lot about people.

Fact: These items do indeed tell a lot about people, their preferences, their religious beliefs, and even their personal eccentricities, but here again the question you must ask yourself is, "Do these things say anything about this person's ability to do the job?" Unless there is an issue of ability, customer service, safety, or hygiene that cannot be handled in another way, you cannot let these elements bias your interview.

INTERVIEWING OBJECTIVELY

Think of a position for which you might be interviewing candidates. What are the skills, abilities, and experience required?

_____

_____

_____

If all candidates have equal skills, abilities, and experience, what other characteristics would be important in making a decision?

➤ Motivated   ➤ Able to communicate with everyone

➤ Hard working   ➤ Honest

➤ Competitive   ➤ Reliable

➤ On time   ➤ Smart

➤ Articulate   ➤ Ability to make decisions

➤ Team player   ➤ Self-directed

➤ Self-reliant   ➤ Passionate about work

What criteria would you use to decide if your candidate has these characteristics? How would you find out if these characteristics show themselves differently in the cultures and values systems of those in your candidate pool? What questions could you ask, and to whom would you speak to make sure?

_____

_____

_____

Without answers to these questions, you are more than likely to choose someone who looks like you or talks or thinks like you, even though that person may not be the most qualified.

Go beyond your usual comfort zones in hiring and view the possibilities other people might bring to the organization. Will you eliminate people just because they do not always look you in the eye?

Questions to Avoid During an Interview

What is asked or stated in an advertisement, on an application, or during an interview can reflect bias and even create legal liability for an organization. These would be statements or questions that have nothing to do with a person's ability to do the job. Here are the most critical ones to avoid:

➤ What is your race?

➤ What is your religion? Do you practice a religion?

➤ Are you a citizen? (It is more helpful to ask whether the person can lawfully work in the country.)

➤ How old are you? When were you born? (If there is a legal age requirement, tell the candidate that proof of age would be required for this job.)

➤ Are you married? What does your spouse do? How do you feel about supervising men/women?

➤ Do you have children? How many children do you have? How old are your children? Do you have arrangements for childcare?

➤ Do you have family concerns that interfere with your ability to travel? (It is illegal to ask questions about family. You can tell candidates that they will need to travel and ask if they are able to do that.)

➤ I see that you have a (for example) Hispanic last name. Do you speak Spanish? (It is illegal to ask about background; you can ask candidates if they speak Spanish if you ask all candidates that question).

➤ How tall are you? What do you weigh (unless this is relevant to the job)?

➤ Do you have any disabilities? (After a conditional job offer, you may require a physical exam to see if an individual is qualified, and then some questions about disability are legitimate.)

➤ Do you belong to a union or have you belonged in the past? How do you feel about unions?

➤ Have you ever been arrested? (A past arrest without conviction does not affect one's ability to do the job; you may ask about a conviction but it is not a reason not to hire unless the conviction relates directly to the job.)

➤ Do you smoke? (But you may point out the company smoking policy.)

It is acceptable and helpful to tell candidates that you have a strong commitment to diversity and to ask how they can help your organization strengthen that commitment.

Finding Employees Who Will Stay Long-Term

Many managers are not trained to interview potential employees from diverse backgrounds. But hiring the wrong person can be expensive. Think about the costs of advertising for candidates, interviewing time, disrupted customer service, training, and severance pay. You want to interview for employees who will stay with your organization.

Pick a position in your organization and estimate how much each step of the hiring process costs in time and money. You will see how important having an interviewing and hiring system is, particularly in this diverse job market. If you do not know how to hire and retain people from diverse backgrounds, you will not only lose money, but you will send talented people to your competition.

Interview Pointers

Creating employee "stickability" for a lower turnover rate begins with finding the right employees for long-term success on the job. Follow these interview pointers to ensure that you—and the candidates—can determine if a good match exists between organization and candidate.

➤ Know your organization:

- Be clear about where your organization is right now and where it is headed in growth and market. This will help you decide what traits and abilities you need for specific positions.
- Decide what environment you want to create, not only for customers, but also for your employee teams. What do your teams look like now? What kind of people do you need to round them out? Do you need a "pusher" to energize the group or a facilitator who can keep team members calm and bring them to consensus?

➤ Know these common candidate selection problems:

- Focusing on only a few critical areas necessary to do the job and not on the whole candidate. You can miss important information about the candidate's experience and skills.
- Disorganized interviewing processes. Use the same selection criteria for all candidates so you can have a baseline for comparing interviewees. Not having a baseline can put some

candidates at a disadvantage, particularly if they are different from you in race, ethnic background, sexual orientation, religion, or age.

- Basing decisions solely on skills without considering motivation. If candidates are not motivated, it does not matter how skilled they are. They will not produce and will likely leave if something better comes along.
- Stereotyping candidates. By letting your biases affect your judgment, you miss out on highly skilled people who can bring new ideas and creativity to your organization.

➤ Know how to interview to find candidates who will stay:

- Ask candidates how they have behaved in specific situations in previous positions. Have them describe specific actions they took and the results. It is not enough for them to say they were part of a team that solved problems. What did they do to help solve a problem?
- Some people come from cultures that are more reluctant to talk about their individual contributions. Phrase your questions about teams, such as "What did you do in the team to help add to its success." Even then, expect understatement.
- How people acted in the past suggests how they will act in the future. Know and ask about situations or tasks that are critical to the position being offered. Vague answers are a warning sign. Ask more specific questions if needed. Behavioral questions help break through bias and stereotypes and allow you to see a person's real ability.
- Use questions that can be answered "yes" or "no" only when you want a quick response. Some cultures say "yes" only to tell you that they heard you. Yes or no questions seldom give you reliable information about the candidate.
- Be clear about the job and its duties, challenges, and future prospects.
- Ask about likes and dislikes as they pertain to the position and the workplace. Candidates whose likes and dislikes conflict with the position's values and needs will make a poor fit.

Introducing New Employees into the Organization

Your job is not done once you have recruited new people. As new employees enter your organization or move from another department, it is your task as manager to integrate them into your team and organizational culture. The faster you can do this, the more quickly they will be able to become fully productive. This is always a challenge because new people bring with them the culture of their old job and their own biases about how to get things done.

How can you best share the culture of your team or organization with new people? How do you let them know about the formal and informal norms that will help them work well in your organization? Follow these five tips:

➤ **Know the local culture.** Do not assume everyone knows the culture of your organization—including yourself. Ask yourself, how is this place different from others in which I have worked? What do outsiders think of us? What can "old-timers" tell you about what has changed since they arrived?

_____

_____

➤ **Spell out unwritten rules.** People may want to know the following points to start working in a new place:

- Is there a dress code? What does it say?
- What do the common TLAs (three-letter abbreviations) mean?
- How do people address each other?
- How do people work together?
- To whom do people go for particular problems?
- What are the major do's and don'ts
- What can you add to the list?

_____

_____

When "breaking in" new people, remember that informal norms about "the way people do things around here" or "how we talk about things" can sometimes be more important than the formal or written rules.

➤ **Encourage questions.** Let new employees know that you are there to answer their questions. When they ask you questions, do not assume they do not know what they are doing. They may just want to figure out the best or most acceptable way to do a particular task.

➤ **Use a buddy system.** See if you can create an informal mentoring or buddy system by assigning an older employee to help a newer one.

➤ **Look for best practices.** When sharing the local culture with others, do not forget to ask them if they are used to doing things differently. The practices new people bring with them may benefit you and your team.

CASE STUDY: MAKING THEM FEEL WELCOME

You are a woman who manages a seafood restaurant chain located on the seacoast of your country. Your headquarters is located in the largest city there. The chain has 30 restaurants, and it is known as a great place to take the whole family for a moderately priced sit-down dinner.

Your company has just bought a smaller chain of Mexican restaurants located in rural areas. You currently manage 22 people at headquarters. Most of them have been with your company at least five years. A week from now two people from the newly acquired restaurant chain will arrive to work at headquarters.

Write out the strategy you will use to integrate the new people into your organization, using the five tips from the preceding section, as follows:

- ❑ Know the local culture
- ❑ Spell out unwritten rules
- ❑ Encourage questions
- ❑ Use a buddy system
- ❑ Look for best practices

How will you get the new employees up to speed in the shortest amount of time and make them feel welcome? What cultural challenges do you expect to face in this case?

_____

_____

_____

Compare your answers to the authors' responses in the Appendix.

Retaining Diverse Talent

After recruiting and hiring your best candidates, you must keep them. If people do not feel welcome or if they believe they have no chance of moving up in your organization because of their race, ethnicity, sexual orientation, gender, or other factor, they will leave and go to a competitor. They will not do their best work. They may file a lawsuit.

At a Fortune 500 company's executive team meeting, a group of white managers said they had come to the realization that they were giving white employees more of a chance to prove themselves and to make mistakes and learn from them without being penalized. They were giving more and better feedback to these employees than they were to their employees of color.

By realizing that hidden assumptions caused them to behave that way, they were able to create better strategies to give all employees an equal chance to show what they could do. Acting on their realization helped them create a more inclusive workplace, increase retention of people of color, and thus bring more people of color—and women—into leadership positions.

Employee Retention in Your Organization

Now think about your own organization and then answer these questions:

➤ What hidden assumptions may be getting in the way of progressing and retaining diverse talent?

➤ What factors may keep these hidden assumptions from being seen and dealt with?

➤ What personal and systemic changes might help your managers and the organization to be more effective in keeping its best and brightest?

Choosing Employees for Promotion

What criteria do you use to decide whether a person should be promoted? It is up to you to advance talented employees—including the person who will be your own successor. There is a paradox here: Managers who make themselves redundant by the effectiveness with which they develop others actually are *unlikely* to become redundant.

It is part of your role to prepare for the future. Get to know your people and their strengths, challenges, and potential as soon as possible. People promoted to management just because they are good at what they do may never have learned to manage people, and they often fail miserably. This is an example of the familiar Peter Principle—employees tend to rise to the level of their incompetence—because although they were good at doing their job, they do not know how to *manage* the people who do that job.[10]

Hand down what you learn to your subordinates. Just as you must learn to overcome biases and assumptions, they too need these skills if they are to lead others. Make sure that requirements for promotion clearly include the ability to:

> ➤ Relate to all kinds of people

> ➤ Identify and help manage conflicts rooted in cultural differences

> ➤ Achieve consensus while encouraging diverse thinking

> ➤ Bring together people with diverse backgrounds, experiences, and talents

> ➤ Facilitate meetings and motivate a diverse team

---

[10] Laurence J. Peter and Raymond Hull, *The Peter Principle, Reissue* (New York: William Morrow & Co., 1996).

Broadening Your Thinking About Managerial Candidates

Diversity is not just about numbers; it is about mobility. An organization whose management consists of a single gender or culture, however varied its employee base, is not a diverse organization. A truly diverse organization respects and uses all the differences that people bring to it. An organization becomes inclusive only when people's differences are represented at all levels.

How can you as a manager expand your thinking about the kind of person it takes to succeed at various management levels? Broaden your outlook by taking the following actions:

❑ Mentor someone from a different culture, ethnic background, or gender.

❑ Identify and supply missing technical skills. Which of your employees have people skills but need extra training to advance in their technical area?

❑ Talk about advancement to those with "people potential." Teach them or help them find what they must learn about their job or technology to go forward.

❑ Model and teach people skills. Many people do the technical side of their jobs faultlessly but need a model and extra attention to develop the people skills to succeed at managing others. Some people learn by being taught; others by watching carefully.

❑ Realize it is up to you to "start the ball rolling." When employees see others like themselves being promoted, it motivates them to succeed. They are also encouraged to support you and others to meet and exceed company or team goals. Their success stories will invite other talent to the organization and take the organization's products or services to a broader market.

❑ Open doors to the future for those you manage. When orienting new hires or conducting performance reviews, ask your people where they would like to go in the company. Help them develop a strategy for getting there. If you do not ask employees what their career goals are, they will focus on limits rather than progress.

❑ Coach those who do not know how to make themselves seen and heard. Many managers make promotion decisions based on informal networking, and they choose people they are most comfortable with or who share their lifestyle. People outside these circles must know how to become active, known, and included. It is a two-way street. Managers must break out of their comfort zone and employees must break in.

CASE STUDY: MICHIKO AND HELEN

Michiko Tanaka was called into her supervisor's office and was told that it was a waste of time for her to apply for a manager's job. Her supervisor, Helen Anderson, said, "You'll never make a good manager. You don't know how to give orders. The only way to be a manager in this place is to tell people what you want them to do and write them up if they don't comply."

Michiko is well respected by the other employees. She is soft spoken, has a slight accent, and believes in asking others for their input in making decisions. Although she has never been given a management job, she has taken responsibility for leading team projects and has always done an outstanding job. Other employees often come to her for advice.

What about your workplace? Do you agree with Helen that to be a successful manager you have to be able to be good at giving orders?

_____

_____

What else makes a manager a good leader? What are the qualities and competencies needed to lead people in your organization?

_____

_____

_____

How would understanding diversity help you as a manager in this situation? How would you coach Helen?

_____

_____

_____

If you were Helen, what coaching would you give Michiko?

_____

_____

_____

Compare your answers to the authors' responses in the Appendix.

Supporting Diverse Leadership Styles

A large international corporation did a cultural audit to find out why women and people of color were leaving the company at a higher rate than other employees. The company wanted to use diversity to gain a competitive edge and widen its customer base. To do that, the company needed a diverse workforce at all levels.

When women and people of color were asked why they were leaving, almost all said they were told that they did not have the right leadership qualities. Many of the people who left went on to become higher-level managers at other companies. The corporation then had a hard time recruiting new women and people of color because of its reputation as a workplace that was not inclusive.

To create an environment that could use diversity to help people do their best work, managers had to rethink their ideas of who would make a good manager and get rid of old ideas about there being only one way to lead. Then they had to start looking more openly to discover who had leadership qualities.

Examining Leadership

List the most important qualities you think a good leader should have:

_____

_____

_____

_____

Who in your organization seems to have these qualities? List them in the left-hand column below.

Persons

_____   _____

_____   _____

_____   _____

Check your list. Are these people primarily from one particular race, ethnic group, or gender? What groups are not represented? Use the right-hand column above to note anything that might tell you how to improve your selection process for a multicultural group.

Different Ways of Leading

In the past, women and people from different ethnic groups were left out of management and leadership positions because their leadership style did not fit a set style or stereotype. Women, for example, tend to use more of a consensus style than men do. In today's workforce, that style is needed along with other styles to create buy-in from employees and to invite feedback and encourage creative ideas.

Now make a new list. Write down the names of employees other than the ones you listed previously. Note in the right-hand column the qualities these people have that might help them lead. Or note how their working or collaboration styles add to your organization.

Persons

_____   _____

_____   _____

_____   _____

Studies show that there is no one best way to lead but that different styles work in different situations and with different people. Think about new ways to lead that you might learn from some of these people and how you might help them use their strengths to benefit your group. Note these in the right-hand column above.

Think about these traits for good leadership in a diverse workplace:

➤ Building relationships

➤ Being able to communicate with a diverse population

➤ Flexibility in solving problems and dealing with employees and customers

➤ Knowing when to listen without giving advice but being willing to give advice when asked for it

➤ Being comfortable with change and knowing when and how to create change

➤ Not being afraid to share power and take suggestions from all organizational levels, from production lines to senior managers

Manager Tip: If there are individuals you think have potential for promotion but are not quite ready, let them know you would like to promote them or give them a leadership role and then help them develop that potential.

Encouraging Input from Everyone on the Team

What can you do to hear from everyone on a diverse team so you do not miss out on more creative ways to solve problems, serve your customers, or develop a better product?

➤ Rather than having the same meeting format every time, try new ways of getting input. Take suggestions from the group. Conduct some meeting where participants are asked to write down their ideas. Then post those ideas and have people discuss them in the large group or in small groups.

➤ Let less outgoing people know that you need their help and would appreciate any ideas they have.

➤ Some people will respond better if not pressured to speak in public. Ask such people for ideas one-on-one.

➤ Some people speak spontaneously; others must think about things first. Always send out agendas in advance. Ask those who need to deliberate to prepare their ideas before the meeting.

➤ Break large groups into smaller, more intimate ones to encourage participation.

➤ Pay attention to the meeting's atmosphere. Make sure the meeting is not seen as a time of criticism, a place where people compete against one another, but as a way to hear from valued colleagues and create new possibilities with them.

CASE STUDY: ENCOURAGING PARTICIPATION AND CREATIVITY

Veronica manages a group of 20 customer service professionals for an organization that builds large computer systems for high-tech companies. She is frustrated by the lack of input and new ideas.

She begins each day with an early-morning meeting of her team to talk about goals, tasks, and client problems. Veronica encourages brainstorming and has set ground rules against judging one another's ideas. She makes sure that everyone's ideas are written down. But the same four people do all the talking and come up with all the ideas.

The team is diverse in ethnic background, age, gender, and professional background. Some speak English as a second language. When given a task, they work without much conflict, but they are not very creative.

Using the points on the preceding page, list obstacles for Veronica to overcome and strategies she could use to get more participation and creativity from her group.

OBSTACLES

_____
_____
_____
_____
_____
_____
_____
_____
_____

STRATEGIES

_____
_____
_____
_____
_____
_____
_____
_____
_____

During the coming week, be aware of how you are asking for input, change the way you conduct your next meeting, and meet one-on-one with someone you have not spoken to very often.

Analyzing Diversity Challenges

Workplace problems and conflicts are inevitable, and they usually involve some element of diversity. Some are diversity issues primarily, while in others diversity adds dimensions or intensity to the situation.

If you are prepared to analyze tough situations, you can help resolve them more quickly. You can also help the stakeholders see and use their diversity to come to better agreement about the present issue and how they will handle future ones.

Here are 10 questions to ask yourself when you want to better understand a problem or conflict involving cultural differences:

➤ Who are the stakeholders in the situation? (List all those affected by it.)

➤ What are the facts in the situation? What is each person specifically doing and saying? What does each stakeholder want or want to have happen?

➤ What are the diversity and cultural issues in this situation? Think about all aspects of diversity.

➤ Which legal or policy issues are involved, if any? Must you do research to be sure you have identified these issues?

➤ What management or organizational concerns are involved?

➤ What do the stakeholders in the situation think, believe, and feel? What individual and group interests are at stake? Have you talked to each person involved to get the necessary information?

➤ What does the situation cost the stakeholders if it is not resolved?

➤ What does the situation cost the organization if it is not resolved? What is the value to the organization if you do resolve the situation?

➤ What steps can be taken to assist the stakeholders to deal with this situation successfully?

➤ What should be done to keep this situation, once resolved, from recurring?

CASE STUDY: PARTNER CARE

As you read the case of Ramón, imagine that this situation is happening in your company or organization. Answer for yourself or discuss with others how you, if you were Ramón, would apply the 10 questions on the preceding page.

Ramón Herrera is a manager in a health-care facility. He has a multicultural team and gets to know each one of his employees. His style is informal and he encourages people to call him by his first name. Ramón is a Cuban American in his mid-40s. He considers himself open-minded and has a collaborative style of managing conflict.

One of his employees is Mark Benson, an African American gay man in his early 50s. Mark has a long-term partner who is seriously ill and needs part-time home care. Ramón has given Mark permission to work from home 16 hours a week. Two of Mark's co-workers, who feel Mark is being treated with favoritism, have expressed resentment.

When leaving work early one day, Mark was in the elevator with Mila Fernandez, a Filipina woman in her late 30s, and James O'Neill, a white man in his 40s. Mila remarked to James, "I wish I got to leave work early, like some people." James replied, "Some people sure know how to work the system here." When Mark tried to talk with them about it, they just ignored him.

Mark went to his manager, Ramón, to ask for help. Mark felt that if people had an issue with him, they should confront him directly. When Ramón spoke with Mila, she denied being resentful and said that in her culture, people did not confront each other directly. Mila still continued to talk about Mark behind his back. James refuses to even communicate with Mark and walks out of the room when Mark enters.

CONTINUED

98

If you were Ramón, how would you analyze this situation? Remember to separate the issues.

What issues are related to diversity?

_____

_____

What issues are just management issues and are not really diversity issues?

_____

_____

What issues are related to productivity?

_____

_____

As a manager, you also must be able to decide what issues must be resolved in the interests of productivity, even though they may seem like diversity issues.

Compare your answers to the authors' responses in the Appendix.

Understanding Conflict Resolution Styles

All workplaces have conflicts. Some are easily resolved before they involve you, but for others you will be called on to mediate. When the conflicts are between people from different cultures or if they involve complaints of harassment, you will not only need to know how to manage conflict, but you will need additional skills as well.

How do you generally respond to conflict? Knowing your own style will keep it from getting in the way of other approaches. Check (✔) how much each of these styles describes you:

Avoid–You tend to back away and pretend you do not even see a problem. This way you can feel that everything in your organization is running smoothly. You find yourself saying, "Just stick to the task and there won't be any problems."

❑ **That's me!**　　❑ **Often**　　❑ **Rarely**　　❑ **Not my style at all**

Accommodate–Because you dislike conflict but cannot always avoid it, you let other people have their way. This way you feel that your team members and employees who report to you will like you. Your other needs are secondary. You might tell yourself that you are keeping all of your employees happy.

❑ **That's me!**　　❑ **Often**　　❑ **Rarely**　　❑ **Not my style at all**

Charge in–It is most important that you are right and that you always prove your point. You often feel that you are in competition with people who disagree with you. It is your way or none at all. You tell yourself and others that you always stand up for what you believe, no matter what.

❑ **That's me!**　　❑ **Often**　　❑ **Rarely**　　❑ **Not my style at all**

Compromise–You are willing to give up some of your needs as long as the other people give up some of theirs. You see this as "meeting other people halfway." Sometimes you give up too much.

❑ **That's me!**　　❑ **Often**　　❑ **Rarely**　　❑ **Not my style at all**

Collaborate–This style has a win-win flavor. You separate people from the problem and partner with others to resolve conflicts and solve problems. You do not take conflict personally and look for the best solutions even if you have to change your original ideas. Everyone ends up benefiting.

❑ **That's me!**　　❑ **Often**　　❑ **Rarely**　　❑ **Not my style at all**

Collaborating to Resolve Conflict

There are times when each of these is appropriate, but collaborating is the preferred American cultural style that is seen as most effective in the majority of conflicts.

Which style do you tend to use more than half the time? That is your preferred style. It is important, though, to understand all five styles because you must be flexible and know when to use each one. You also must recognize the styles in others.

Get comfortable with the collaborative process and be able to use it even if you choose another method to resolve the issue. In other words, do not personalize the conflict even if it involves you. Separate the people from the problem, and find a resolution that is in the best interests of the team.

Managing People in Conflict

Once you are comfortable with collaboration, you are ready for the next step in facilitating conflict between people of different races, ethnicity, gender, sexual orientation, work level, and so on. Read through the conflict resolution behaviors below. Ignore the boxes and circles for now.

1. Listen to both sides with an open mind. Be conscious of your biases and the judgments you tend to make based on them. ❏ ◯

2. Make sure you give all parties a chance to speak without being interrupted. ❏ ◯

3. Look at whoever is speaking and be aware of your non-verbal cues. Make sure you face the speaker, look interested, and give all parties the same amount of attention as they speak. ❏ ◯

4. Let people know the ground rules before you get started, such as taking turns and not interrupting. ❏ ◯

5. Wait for each person to finish talking. Do not let your facial expressions or gestures display annoyance, irritation, or disagreement. ❏ ◯

6. Avoid favoring one person over another, regardless if one of the parties is a friend of yours, is from a culture you are more comfortable with, or simply appeals to you more. ❏ ◯

7. Do not assume that people who are more verbal than others or more comfortable speaking in front of others are more credible or right. ❏ ◯

8. Ask open-ended questions when getting the facts. Encourage each person to give as much detail as possible. ❏ ◯

9. Put yourself in each person's frame of mind to see another point of view. ❏ ◯

10. Decide when to talk to people separately and when to bring them together, depending on the situation. ❏ ◯

11. Avoid criticizing people for being emotional. Instead, suggest that they speak more calmly so they can hear each other better. ❏ ◯

12. Do not suggest people look each other in the eye or try to resolve it themselves. They are looking to you as an outside party. ❏ ◯

13. Ask for outside help when you need it. ❏ ◯

Conflict Resolution in Practice

Think about a recent conflict or disagreement that you mediated that was a success for all parties involved. Which of the behaviors in the list on the previous page were key to your success? Put a check (✔) in the box after them.

Second, think of a less successful situation in which you took part. Which of these behaviors were missing or done poorly? Check (✔) the circle behind those behaviors. Do this now.

Look at the pattern of behaviors that you checked for each situation. Compare the two and in the space below, write any conclusions or lessons you see for future conflict management.

_____

_____

_____

_____

Dealing with Sexual Harassment

What do you do when one of your employees accuses another of harassment? As a manager, the more informed you are, the better your chances of dealing with it effectively.

Workplace aggression can take many forms, including racial, age, gender, national origin, disability, and religious harassment. Harassment also includes harmful behaviors such as stalking and mobbing, or frequent harassment, "torment," or discrimination and exclusion in the workplace by colleagues or superiors over a long period. This section will look at sexual harassment specifically because it is most detailed.

Defining Sexual Harassment

Sexual harassment in the United States is defined by the EEOC as "unwelcome sexual advances, requests for sexual favors, and other verbal or physical conduct of a sexual nature when" any of the following conditions are present:

> ➤ Submitting to such conduct is made either explicitly or implicitly a term or condition of an individual's employment

> ➤ Submitting to or rejecting such conduct by an individual is used as a basis for employment decisions affecting the individual

> ➤ Such conduct has the purpose or effect of unreasonably interfering with an individual's work performance or creating an intimidating, hostile, or offensive working environment.

Preparing for Harassment Complaints

Learning in advance what to do should an employee raise a harassment complaint will help you deal with the complaint more effectively when the time comes. Follow these steps to prepare:

> ➤ Understand and be able to discuss with your employees all aspects of the laws on sexual harassment and discrimination in title VII. Do not leave everything up to your human resources department.

> ➤ Know your organizations' policies and procedures about sexual harassment and discrimination. Too many managers are not prepared and wait until they have a complaint before they learn what they must do.

➤ Understand your legal obligations and responsibilities as a manager.

➤ Listen to complainants with an open mind. Try to see their point of view, particularly if they are of a different gender or culture than you. Remember, just because it may not seem like a big deal to you does not mean that it is not harassment.

Many managers have a hard time dealing with harassment complaints when the accused is a friend of theirs or is of a similar background. Knowing individuals personally can make it hard for you to imagine their exhibiting harassing behavior if you have not seen that side of them. If they are from your own ethnic or racial background, it can be hard to be objective because of how you may be received by other members of your group.

Fostering a Harassment-Free Workplace

Everyone has a right to work in an environment free of harassment. If someone is harassed, it can have a negative effect on the whole environment. Individuals being harassed cannot work at their best level. If nothing is done about the harasser and everyone sees it, the whole team is demoralized.

If you have a human resources department, you do not have to solve the whole problem yourself, but you have to be willing to deal with it and support the accuser if the claims prove valid.

As a manager who values diversity and the benefits it brings to your workplace, you must provide an environment where people are comfortable speaking with you about work-related issues without fear of retaliation or exclusion.

The best way to handle harassment is prevention. Educate yourself. Then educate your employees. Show appropriate behavior in the workplace by example. Refuse to collude with potential harassers and do not laugh at or allow sexual or racial jokes in your workplace. Demonstrate respect for the work of all employees and pay attention to reports of inappropriate behavior.

CASE STUDY: STALKING AND UNWANTED GIFTS

Think through the steps you would take to help solve the following harassment problem between Mary and Victor.

You are the manager of a 25-person department. Rosalind Johnson tells you that Victor Mikulski is verbally harassing Mary Huang. Victor has tried to get Mary to go out with him and will not listen when she says no. He has begun to stalk her after work by calling her at home and sending her unwanted gifts. Rosalind tells you that Mary is having a hard time staying focused on her work. When you ask Rosalind why Mary has not said anything, Rosalind says that she tried talking to Mary, but was told that she is concerned about bringing shame to herself and her family. (Mary is a first-generation Chinese American.) Mary is also afraid of losing her job if she complains.

How would you handle this situation?

_____

_____

What information do you need to be able to make a decision?

_____

_____

What kind of help can you seek to resolve this?

_____

_____

What steps would you take?

_____

_____

Should you approach Mary and if so, what would you say?

_____

_____

How would you deal with the cultural issues?

_____

_____

Compare your answers to the authors' responses in the Appendix.

Progress Check

Part 4 has provided you with many challenges you may face as you strive to diversify your workplace successfully. Do a spot summary of what you have learned.

1. I have a better idea of how to map and analyze a diversity challenge.

    ❑ **Yes**   ❑ **I need to pay attention to** _____

2. I understand my own style of reacting to conflict better, and steps to take when faced with conflict.

    ❑ **Yes**   ❑ **I need to pay attention to** _____

3. I feel I can interview diverse employees more effectively and more sensitively.

    ❑ **Yes**   ❑ **I need to pay attention to** _____

4. I have a better sense of what it takes to encourage, retain, and promote good employees from backgrounds different from my own.

    ❑ **Yes**   ❑ **I need to pay attention to** _____

5. I understand the nature of harassment and am willing and prepared to respond to it.

    ❑ **Yes**   ❑ **I need to pay attention to** _____

Congratulations on having completed this workbook. We wish you success in your diversity efforts and applaud your commitment to making your people and your organization succeed and contribute to a more equitable, peaceful, and productive world.

A P P E N D I X

Authors' Suggested Responses

Part 2: Developing Yourself

Progress Check (Page 47)

1. Diversity addresses the multitude of differences that lead people to think and act differently. It includes men and women, and it addresses backgrounds of all types, not just ethnic backgrounds.

2. To make sense of the world, we prejudge certain things. Our minds are not 100% accurate, so we carry around biases and assumptions that are incorrect. Your best defense against your own prejudices and assumptions is to consciously seek out information to help you analyze and address them.

3. It may fall to the human resources department to hire a diverse workforce in some organizations, but it is your responsibility to be a diversity leader. You have the ability and responsibility for creating a workplace culture that supports diversity and social harmony.

4. Diversity creates compassion, cooperation, understanding, and innovation. Organizations need these elements and will continue to benefit from the value diversity brings to the workplace. Diversity training will continue to be an important step to ensuring these outcomes and will only become more important in the age of globalization.

5. Following laws that pertain to a diverse workforce is part, not all, of managing diversity. The more you support a culture of diversity in your organization, the less you will rely on these laws.

6. People are not the same, so treating them the same ignores their diversity.

7. We are currently separated by our differences. Knowing and respecting them brings us together. Acknowledging our differences often makes it easier to communicate with one another and discover our real similarities.

Part 4: Diversifying Your Workplace Successfully

Case Study: Making Them Feel Welcome (Page 86)

As a restaurant manager, what would you do?

Make a list of all the formal and informal norms and written and unwritten rules in your organization and department. Include information about your work group's culture, such as dress-down Fridays, monthly potluck lunches, and the ways people address each other. Write down the commonly used acronyms and their meanings, and whom to go to for advice and feedback on particular issues or problems. By providing this information, you can save time for a new person and money for your organization.

This will also help new people feel included and welcome. Give them a list of places of interest in your city and assign someone from your work group to orient them around the building and help them learn the basics about your restaurant culture. Make a list of questions that you might want to ask them about their old company and about working in its headquarters. Some of the cultural issues will be around change in geography, urban vs. rural, sit-down family restaurant vs. fast food, and seafood vs. Mexican cuisines.

Get local employees involved in thinking this through and helping to welcome and inform the newcomers as well as learning about them. They will learn about themselves in the process and feel less threatened by the newcomers.

As you get all of this done, imagine yourself as a new person in your organization. Think of what else you might need to be comfortable and productive, and include those items in your list. What is critical here is not only the information you give, but also the sense of welcome and support that you convey to both newcomers and old-timers.

Case Study: Michiko and Helen (Page 90)

What coaching does each of them need?

Perhaps Helen succeeded in her own career by learning to give orders in a workplace that saw this as the best way to lead. If so, it is important for her to tell Michiko that more assertiveness may be required of her if she receives a promotion. Certainly if she has the will to ask for a promotion, she has motivation and resources to learn what is needed in a new role.

Just as anyone can learn a new language when necessary, we can learn to step out of our cultural and personal conditioning to behave and succeed in new ways, especially if we have good coaching and support. It may not be easy or feel right at first, but being in a diverse workplace challenges all of us to stretch a bit.

Helen should not be seen as a hopeless case either. She needs to take a good look at what skills Michiko brings to her teamwork and informal leadership. Certainly there are many ways to manage and lead, and a diverse organization will need more than one way to get the best out of its people. Helen can become a better manager if she sees what her subordinates do well but differently from herself. She may even learn from them. And the managers to whom she reports should support her in this.

Case Study: Partner Care (Page 97–98)

If you were Ramón, what would you do?

The main diversity issue is that Mark is being allowed to work at home to help take care of his ill partner. This shows a commitment to diversity and helping people do their best work. Ramón, the manager, must deal with the resentment and comments made by Mila and James, and find the causes of the resentment.

If working from home for caregiving is already accepted in the organization, then possibly James and Mila are at least unconsciously responding out of racial bias or homophobia. In any case, Ramón needs to tell his employees the company policy on work-at-home programs and caring for ill partners and family members. Management must address Mila's comments and James' behavior toward Mark. The two must be told that their conduct and rude remarks are unacceptable.

Mila said she did not talk with Mark about his working at home because in her culture people do not confront each other directly, but her behavior toward Mark is inappropriate in the workplace and is in fact confrontational. Although indirectness may be part of her cultural heritage, she seems in this situation to be "playing a cultural card" to cover poor behavior.

This might also be a clue that Ramón must improve his communication with his employees and among the employees themselves. If unresolved, this and similar issues will affect both morale and productivity.

Case Study: Stalking and Unwanted Gifts (Page 105)

As manager of a 25-person department, what would you do?

You must address your responsibilities as a manager and also you must be clear on the law. You must be concerned about all your employees—Victor and Mary and the people around them who might be affected by what is taking place. Not only must Victor understand that his behavior makes him a harasser at work, but also that he may even be brought up on criminal charges for stalking. If you do nothing, you can be liable, particularly if any physical harm comes to Mary. Inaction on your part will lower other employees' morale and sense of safety.

Recommended Reading

Farrell, Warren. *The Myth of Male Power.* New York: Penguin USA, 2001.

Harris, Philip R., and Robert T. Moran. *Managing Cultural Differences, Fifth Edition.* Woburn, MA: Butterworth-Heinemann, 2000.

Laroche, Lionel, PhD. *Managing Cultural Diversity in Technical Professions.* Woburn, MA: Butterworth-Heinemann, 2002.

Maalouf, Amin. *In the Name of Identity: Violence and the Need to Belong.* New York: Penguin USA, 2003.

Myers, Selma, and Barbara Filner. *Conflict Resolution Across Cultures: From Talking It Out to Third Party Mediation.* Amherst, MA: Amherst Educational Publishing, 1997.

Pollard, Odette and Raphael Gonzalez. *Dynamics of Diversity: Strategic Programs for Your Organization.* Menlo Park, CA: Crisp Publications, 1994.

Rosen, Robert H., Carl Phillips, and Patricia Digh. *Global Literacies: Lessons on Business Leadership and National Cultures.* New York: Simon & Schuster, 2000.

Rosinski, Philippe. *Coaching Across Cultures: New Tools for Leveraging National, Corporate, and Professional Differences.* London: Nicholas Brealey Publishers, and Yarmouth, ME: Intercultural Press, 2002.

Simons, George. *Working Together: Succeeding in a Multicultural Organization, Revised Edition.* Menlo Park, CA: Crisp Publications, 2003.

Additional Resources

The organizations listed here are sources of diversity-related products and services.

Castle Consultants International cooperates with George Simons International to provide training in communicating and negotiating across cultures in Europe. http://www.castles.co.uk

George Simons International is a worldwide network of established professionals providing assessment, consulting, and training in cultural and gender diversity and virtual global teamwork. Specializing in intercultural expertise online, the network developed the DIVERSOPHY® intercultural training game and a wide variety of diversity publications, tools, and instruments. http://www.diversophy.com

Managing Diversity Newsletter is a monthly publication in which top diversity experts offer ideas and practical suggestions for how to manage the multicultural workforce. http://www.jalmc.org/mg-diver.htm

ODT Inc. is a source of articles, tip sheets, reprints, materials, and training programs on cultural diversity. It features a resource collection of books, audiotapes, articles, pamphlets, catalogs, and maps. Telephone: 800-736-1293 http://www.odt.org & http://www.petersmap.com

Peralta Associates provides your workforce with practical, hands-on skills and knowledge that facilitate communication in culturally diverse environments, in the United States and abroad. http://www.peraltaassociates.com

Simma Lieberman Associates specializes in diversity, gender communication, and life/work balance, providing training, consulting, and speaking services to create environments where people can do their best work and enjoy what they do. http://www.simmalieberman.com

For regularly updated list of online resources, please go to http://www.diversophy.com/putdiv2work

115

Resources available from www.diversophy.com:

Simons, George F., ed. *EuroDiversity: A Business Guide to Managing Differences.* Oxford, England, and Woburn, MA: Butterworth-Heinemann, 2002.

Simons, George F., and Dr. Bob Abramms. *Cultural Diversity Sourcebook.* Amherst, MA: HRD Press, 1996.

Simons, George F., and Dr. Bob Abramms. *Cultural Diversity Supplement #1,* 1996.

Simons, George F., and Bob Abramms, eds. *The Questions of Diversity: Assessment Tools for Organizations & Individuals, Fifth Edition.* Amherst, MA: HRD Press, 1994.

Simons, George F., Dr. Bob Abramms, and L. Ann Hopkins with Diane Johnson. *Cultural Diversity Fieldbook.* 1996.

Simons, George F., Selma Myers, and Jonamay Lambert, eds. *Global Competence: 50 Exercises for Succeeding in International Business.* Amherst, MA: HRD Press, 2000.

Simons, George F., Carmen Vazquez, and Philip R. Harris. *Transcultural Leadership: Empowering the Diverse Workforce.* Woburn, MA: Butterworth-Heinemann, 1993.

Simons, George F., and Amy J. Zuckerman. *Sexual Orientation in the Workplace.* Thousand Oaks, CA: Sage Publications, 1994.

DIVERSOPHY® Training Games

U.S. Domestic DIVERSOPHY®
The original U.S. workplace game designed to address U.S. workforce and organizational diversity issues. Developed by George Simons and edited by Amy Zuckerman; updated by Brooke Smith.

HealthCare I and II
Addresses the medical wellness concerns and habits of major U.S. ethnic groups. Developed by Suzanne Salimbene and edited by George Simons.

U.S. Gender Diversity
Addresses gender and sexual harassment issues in the U.S. workplace. Developed by George Simons and Amy Zuckerman.

diversiPLAY
Sixty workplace role-play situations for use with board game or separately. Developed by George Simons.

Managing Ability
Addresses abilities issues in the workplace and the consequences of the Americans with Disabilities Act. Developed and edited by George Simons.

DIVERSOPHY® Canada
Deals with domestic Canadian diversity. Developed by Laura Sarino and Hilary Ottley and edited by George Simons.

Now Available From

Books•Videos•CD-ROMs•Computer-Based Training Products

Subject Areas Include:

Management

Human Resources

Communication Skills

Personal Development

Marketing/Sales

Organizational Development

Customer Service/Quality

Computer Skills

Small Business and Entrepreneurship

Adult Literacy and Learning

Life Planning and Retirement

CRISP WORLDWIDE DISTRIBUTION

English language books are distributed worldwide. Major international distributors include:

ASIA/PACIFIC

Australia/New Zealand: In Learning, PO Box 1051, Springwood QLD, Brisbane, Australia 4127   Tel: 61-7-3-841-2286, Facsimile: 61-7-3-841-1580
ATTN: Messrs. Richard/Robert Gordon

Hong Kong/Mainland China: Crisp Learning Solutions, 18/F Honest Motors Building 9-11 Leighton Road, Causeway Bay, Hong Kong   Tel: 852-2915-7119, Facsimile: 852-2865-2815 ATTN: Ms. Grace Lee

Indonesia: Pt Lutan Edukasi, Citra Graha, 7th Floor, Suite 701A, Jl. Jend. Gato Subroto Kav. 35-36, Jakarta 12950 Indonesia Tel: 62-21-527-9060/527-9061 Facsimile: 62-21-527-9062 ATTN: Mr. Suwardi Luis

Japan: Phoenix Associates, Believe Mita Bldg., 8th Floor 3-43-16 Shiba, Minato-ku, Tokyo 105-0014, Japan   Tel: 81-3-5427-6231, Facsimile: 81-3-5427-6232
ATTN: Mr. Peter Owans

Malaysia, Philippines, Singapore: Epsys Pte Ltd., 540 Sims Avenue #04-01, Sims Avenue Centre, 387603, Singapore   Tel: 65-747-1964, Facsimile: 65-747-0162 ATTN: Mr. Jack Chin

CANADA

Crisp Learning Canada, 60 Briarwood Avenue, Mississauga, ON L5G 3N6 Canada
Tel: 905-274-5678, Facsimile: 905-278-2801 ATTN: Mr. Steve Connolly

EUROPEAN UNION

England: Flex Learning Media, Ltd., 9-15 Hitchin Street,
Baldock, Hertfordshire, SG7 6AL, England
Tel: 44-1-46-289-6000, Facsimile: 44-1-46-289-2417   ATTN: Mr. David Willetts

INDIA

Multi-Media HRD, Pvt. Ltd., National House, Floor 1, 6 Tulloch Road,
Appolo Bunder, Bombay, India 400-039 Tel: 91-22-204-2281,
Facsimile: 91-22-283-6478 ATTN: Messrs. Ajay Aggarwal/ C.L. Aggarwal

SOUTH AMERICA

Mexico: Grupo Editorial Iberoamerica, Nebraska 199, Col. Napoles, 03810 Mexico, D.F.
Tel: 525-523-0994, Facsimile: 525-543-1173   ATTN: Señor Nicholas Grepe

SOUTH AFRICA

Corporate: Learning Resources, PO Box 2806, Parklands, Johannesburg 2121, South Africa, Tel: 27-21-531-2923, Facsimile: 27-21-531-2944 ATTN: Mr. Ricky Robinson

MIDDLE EAST

Edutech Middle East, L.L.C., PO Box 52334, Dubai U.A.E.
Tel: 971-4-359-1222, Facsimile: 971-4-359-6500   ATTN: Mr. A.S.F. Karim